CONTENTS

S. HRG. 108–217

CONSTITUTIONALISM, HUMAN RIGHTS, AND THE RULE OF LAW IN IRAQ

JOINT HEARING

BEFORE THE

SUBCOMMITTEE ON NEAR EASTERN AND SOUTH ASIAN AFFAIRS

OF THE

COMMITTEE ON FOREIGN RELATIONS
UNITED STATES SENATE

AND THE

SUBCOMMITTEE ON THE CONSTITUTION, CIVIL RIGHTS AND PROPERTY RIGHTS

OF THE

COMMITTEE ON THE JUDICIARY
UNITED STATES SENATE

ONE HUNDRED EIGHTH CONGRESS

FIRST SESSION

JUNE 25, 2003

Printed for the use of the Committee on Foreign Relations

Available via the World Wide Web: http://www.access.gpo.gov/congress/senate

U.S. GOVERNMENT PRINTING OFFICE
90–493 PDF WASHINGTON : 2003

For sale by the Superintendent of Documents, U.S. Government Printing Office
Internet: bookstore.gpo.gov Phone: toll free (866) 512–1800; DC area (202) 512–1800
Fax: (202) 512–2250 Mail: Stop SSOP, Washington, DC 20402–0001

COMMITTEE ON FOREIGN RELATIONS

RICHARD G. LUGAR, Indiana, *Chairman*

CHUCK HAGEL, Nebraska
LINCOLN CHAFEE, Rhode Island
GEORGE ALLEN, Virginia
SAM BROWNBACK, Kansas
MICHAEL B. ENZI, Wyoming
GEORGE V. VOINOVICH, Ohio
LAMAR ALEXANDER, Tennessee
NORM COLEMAN, Minnesota
JOHN E. SUNUNU, New Hampshire

JOSEPH R. BIDEN, JR., Delaware
PAUL S. SARBANES, Maryland
CHRISTOPHER J. DODD, Connecticut
JOHN F. KERRY, Massachusetts
RUSSELL D. FEINGOLD, Wisconsin
BARBARA BOXER, California
BILL NELSON, Florida
JOHN D. ROCKEFELLER IV, West Virginia
JON S. CORZINE, New Jersey

KENNETH A. MYERS, JR., *Staff Director*
ANTONY J. BLINKEN, *Democratic Staff Director*

SUBCOMMITTEE ON NEAR EASTERN AND SOUTH ASIAN AFFAIRS

LINCOLN CHAFEE, Rhode Island, *Chairman*

CHUCK HAGEL, Nebraska
SAM BROWNBACK, Kansas
GEORGE V. VOINOVICH, Ohio
NORM COLEMAN, Minnesota

BARBARA BOXER, California
JON S. CORZINE, New Jersey
JOHN D. ROCKEFELLER IV, West Virginia
PAUL S. SARBANES, Maryland

COMMITTEE ON THE JUDICIARY

ORRIN G. HATCH, Utah, *Chairman*

CHARLES E. GRASSLEY, Iowa
ARLEN SPECTER, Pennsylvania
JON KYL, Arizona
MIKE DEWINE, Ohio
JEFF SESSIONS, Alabama
LINDSEY O. GRAHAM, South Carolina
LARRY E. CRAIG, Idaho
SAXBY CHAMBLISS, Georgia
JOHN CORNYN, Texas

PATRICK J. LEAHY, Vermont
EDWARD M. KENNEDY, Massachusetts
JOSEPH R. BIDEN, JR., Delaware
HERBERT KOHL, Wisconsin
DIANNE FEINSTEIN, California
RUSSELL D. FEINGOLD, Wisconsin
CHARLES E. SCHUMER, New York
RICHARD J. DURBIN, Illinois
JOHN EDWARDS, North Carolina

MAKAN DELRAHIM, *Chief Counsel and Staff Director*
BRUCE A. COHEN, *Democratic Chief Counsel and Staff Director*

SUBCOMMITTEE ON THE CONSTITUTION, CIVIL RIGHTS AND PROPERTY RIGHTS

JOHN CORNYN, Texas, *Chairman*

JON KYL, Arizona
LINDSEY O. GRAHAM, South Carolina
LARRY E. CRAIG, Idaho
SAXBY CHAMBLISS, Georgia

RUSSELL D. FEINGOLD, Wisconsin
EDWARD M. KENNEDY, Massachusetts
CHARLES E. SCHUMER, New York
RICHARD J. DURBIN, Illinois

JAMES C. HO, *Majority Chief Counsel*
ROBERT F. SCHIFF, *Democratic Chief Counsel*

CONSTITUTIONALISM, HUMAN RIGHTS, AND THE RULE OF LAW IN IRAQ

Wednesday, June 25, 2003

U.S. SENATE,
SUBCOMMITTEE ON NEAR EASTERN AND
SOUTH ASIAN AFFAIRS,
Committee on Foreign Relations

SUBCOMMITTEE ON THE CONSTITUTION,
CIVIL RIGHTS AND PROPERTY RIGHTS,
Committee on the Judiciary,
Washington, D.C.

The subcommittees met, pursuant to notice, at 2:13 p.m. in room SD–226, Dirksen Senate Office Building, Hon. John Cornyn, chairman of the Subcommittee on the Constitution, Civil Rights and Property Rights, Committee on the Judiciary, and Hon. Lincoln Chafee, chairman of the Subcommittee on Near Eastern and South Asian Affairs, Committee on Foreign Relations, presiding.

Present: Senators Cornyn, Chafee, and Feingold.

OPENING STATEMENT OF HON. JOHN CORNYN, U.S. SENATOR FROM TEXAS

Senator CORNYN. This joint hearing of the Senate Judiciary Subcommittee on the Constitution, Civil Rights and Property Rights and the Senate Foreign Relations Subcommittee on Near Eastern and South Asian Affairs shall come to order.

In a moment I want to begin my opening statement and then turn the floor over to Senator Chafee, the chairman of the Foreign Relations subcommittee, and then to my ranking member, Senator Feingold, and Senator Boxer, the ranking minority Member of Senator Chafee's committee, but I want to first express my appreciation to Chairman Hatch and also to Chairman Lugar, who is the chairman of the Senate Foreign Relations Committee, as well as Senators Biden, obviously Senators Chafee and Boxer for all the hard work that they've done and their staffs have done to make sure that this hearing could proceed today.

It is my honor to join Chairman Chafee in opening our joint subcommittee hearing this afternoon on the issue of constitutionalism, human rights, and the rule of law in Iraq.

Today, the lights are back on in Baghdad. The sound of gunfire is still there, but not quite so loud as before. The climate in Iraq can best be described as cautious unease. The Iraqi people today are free of Saddam, but they are not yet free of fear. We've seen progress when it comes to ensuring the basic security of the Iraqi people, the recruitment of a new police force, the continued elimination of Ba'athist party remnants, and the capture of armed gangs of militants, all of which are positive signs, but clearly there is a lot more that needs to be done.

We must end the looting and the street violence and restore the rights of the Iraqi people. The foundation of a peaceful, just, and prosperous society cannot be constructed while lawlessness reigns. The current unstable situation is at least in part, I believe, an unintended by-product of the swiftness and efficiency of our own military forces and coalition forces. Never before has the world witnessed such a marvel of technology, training, dedication, and leadership in war, and I am enormously proud of our heroic men and women in uniform who bravely put themselves at risk for the cause of freedom.

Yet currently, the only thing that prevents the mass outbreak of conflict by Iraq's rival ethnic and religious groups is the authority of coalition military forces. This stop gap is clearly no substitute for long-term solutions. The Iraqi people must relearn how to govern themselves and police themselves.

We can harbor no illusions about the reconstruction of Iraq. The current occupation will not and perhaps should not be brief. While the administration understandably wants to return Iraq to the Iraqi people as soon as possible, this well-intentioned desire could backfire. Iraq looks a lot like the Old West right now, and we need lawmen to restore peace and to protect the populace. In my State, the Texas Rangers have a saying, "One Ranger, One Riot," but Iraq will need more than just one police officer, one Ranger. It will need a substantial professional and civilian police force untainted by Saddam's enforcers.

I am delighted to be able to co-chair this hearing with Senator Chafee, and I want to make sure we have plenty of time to hear from my colleagues here during their opening statements, and so I'm going to submit the rest of my opening statement for the record, but one of the things that I hope we achieve here today is that we have intelligent discourse and exchange on what post-war reconstruction looks like in Iraq from people who are really world-recognized experts in various aspects of, either that of geographical location and the culture and the history of the Iraqi people, or others who are experts in the law, who can help illuminate, I think, a civil discourse on what it will take to establish the rule of law in Iraq, and hopefully help the Iraqi people nurture a democratic, representative government in that nation.

With that, let me please turn the floor over to my co-chair for the purposes of this hearing, Senator Lincoln Chafee.

STATEMENT OF HON. LINCOLN D. CHAFEE, U.S. SENATOR FROM RHODE ISLAND

Senator CHAFEE. Thank you very much, Senator Cornyn. It's a pleasure to co-chair this hearing with you this afternoon, and welcome the distinguished panelists who have taken their valuable time to be here with us also this afternoon.

A few weeks ago, May 22 in particular, Deputy Secretary of Defense Paul Wolfowitz appeared before the Foreign Relations Committee and I asked him, what are the effects of what we have done in Iraq, and he said three things in particular. The first is, he thought it would have a positive impact on the Israeli-Palestinian peace process. Second, he thought it would improve the strategic position of Saudi Arabia and other moderate Arab countries in the region, and third, he said it would bring us to a point where Iraq could be a model of democracy in the Arab world, and that's why we're here this afternoon, to see that process started which, of course, the first step is to have a constitution, and I look forward to hearing from the distinguished people who will advise us on the process to go forward in establishing a constitution for Iraq as the first step to democracy.

I did notice from Dr. El Fadl's submitted written testimony I think something that's very true, and he said, the worst thing that the Government of the United States could possibly do while acting as an occupying power in Iraq is to impose upon the Iraqi people a political condition that is so artificial, that is so alien to the collective consciousness of the Iraqis, that it is at odds with the historical experience and aspirations, that it appears that the United States is, in fact, acting like a power of occupation and domination, not persuasion and liberation.

The danger is that if the United States appears hostile or insensitive to the religious sentiments of the Iraqis, this will invite resistance. It would be a real tragedy if the democratic experiment in Iraq fails, not because the Iraqis do not believe in democracy but because democracy is seen as part of an ideological package of an aggressive or imperialistic occupying force, and I think that's the most important thing.

What a tragedy it would be if democracy fails because we didn't do it right, and of course the first step is to get a good constitution, and I look forward to the testimony as we go forward.

Senator CORNYN. Thank you, Senator Chafee, and now I'd like to turn the floor over to the ranking member of the Constitution Subcommittee, Senator Russ Feingold, who has worked with us, he and his staff, to prepare this hearing today, and Senator Feingold, I'll turn it over to you.

Senator FEINGOLD. Thank you, Mr. Chairman. First let me ask, Senator Boxer has asked that her statement be submitted for the record.

Senator CORNYN. Without objection.

[The prepared statement of Senator Boxer follows:]

STATEMENT SUBMITTED BY SENATOR BARBARA BOXER

Chairman Chafee, Chairman Cornyn, thank you for holding this hearing today on Constitutionalism, Human Rights and the Rule of Law in the Nation of Iraq.

The Senate Foreign Relations Committee has held several hearings on Iraq since last July, beginning under the leadership of Chairman Biden and then under Chairman Lugar. In February, prior to U.S. military action against Iraq, the committee held a hearing on post-Saddam Iraq. Representatives of both the State Department and Department of Defense testified.

The committee asked several questions:

Who will rule Iraq?

Who will provide security?

How long will U.S. troops have to say?

What will be the role of the U.N.?

What allies will share the burden of reconstructing Iraq?

During this hearing, the committee failed to get clear answers—only rosy scenarios. As Chairman Lugar recently said, "We were unable in this committee to find very much from the administration about what they were going to do." The administration—in the Chairman's own words—was not "well prepared."

In my view, the number one priority in Iraq is to provide basic law and order. It is unfortunate that we were not better prepared to stop the looting and lawlessness that took place after the fall of Baghdad.

Now, our military men and women, who so ably fought to rid Iraq of Saddam Hussein, are frustrated that they have not been given the tools or training to act as peacekeepers.

According to the *Washington Post,* "soldiers complain that they have been insufficiently equipped for peacekeeping and too thinly deployed in areas where they are under attack from fighters evidently loyal to deposed president Saddam Hussein."

Because of the Bush administration's insistence on a unilateral policy toward Iraq, the task of keeping peace falls almost exclusively to the United States. Right now, the U.S. has 146,000 troops in Iraq—non-U.S. coalition forces number 12,000. U.S. forces make up 92 percent of the total. To compare, after hostilities ended in Bosnia, the security force was about one-third American; in Kosovo, about one-fifth. It is imperative that we do more to involve other nations in maintaining law and order in Iraq.

A second issue we face is how to establish a viable transitional government of Iraq. It is clear that the administration's initial plans have failed. General Gamer has been recalled and replaced by a civilian administrator. The Pentagon's plan to give power to Mr. Chalabi and the Iraqi National Congress has apparently been scrapped.

Unlike Afghanistan where a Loya Jirga allowed Hamid Karzai to take control relatively soon after the fall of the Taliban, no such mechanism to produce a viable Iraqi leader has emerged.

Finally, I want to highlight the need to ensure that our initial missteps in Iraq do not lead to a rise in religious fundamentalism. In yesterday's *New York Times,* Nicolas Kristof writes that, "An iron curtain of fundamentalism risks falling over Iraq, with particularly grievous implications for girls and women. President Bush hopes that Iraq will turn into a shining model of democracy, and that could still happen. But for now it's the Shiite fundamentalists who are gaining ground."

Concerns about women and girls led me to offer an amendment to the Foreign Assistance Authorization bill to make it U.S. policy to ensure the full and active participation of women in the reconstruction of Iraq by promoting the involvement of women in the Iraqi government, the planning and distribution of assistance, and job promotion and training programs. I am pleased this amendment was unanimously adopted by the Foreign Relations Committee.

In addition, a report is being released today by Women Waging Peace in conjunction with the Woodrow Wilson Center on the role of women in post-conflict Iraq. The findings contained in this report are the result of a two-day conference involving 26 Iraqi women leaders. Zainab Salbi, who will testify as part of our first panel of witnesses this afternoon, played a key role in the development of this report.

We must ensure the full and active participation of women in the rebuilding of Iraq. It is necessary for long-term stability and the success of a democratic transition.

Thank you.

STATEMENT OF HON. RUSSELL D. FEINGOLD, U.S. SENATOR FROM WISCONSIN

Senator FEINGOLD. Thank you, Mr. Chairman.

Chairman Chafee and Chairman Cornyn, as you know, not only am I fortunate to be the ranking member of the Constitution Subcommittee, but I'm also a member of the Foreign Relations Committee. In that capacity, I've attended every Foreign Relations Committee hearing on Iraq over the past year, going all the way back to Chairman Biden's first hearings on Iraq in late July and early August of 2002.

Those hearings which were held before, during, and now after the war with Iraq have explored a wide variety of issues, including a series of hearings focused on aspects of stabilization and reconstruction from the regional repercussions of changes in Iraq to international contributions to this post-conflict effort.

While the Foreign Relations Committee is very active in overseeing assistance designed to strengthen the rule of law and legal institutions around the world, one issue it has not yet explored in depth is the issue we will discuss today, establishing the rule of law in Iraq, so I commend the chairmen of the two subcommittees, Senators Chafee and Cornyn, for their leadership in calling this hearing. I'd also like to thank the chairman, as well as Senators Lugar, Biden, and Boxer and their staffs for their cooperation and collaboration in organizing this hearing.

The purpose of this hearing is to explore some of the challenges the Iraqi people will face in reaching their goal of a stable and just society that respects basic human rights, including the rights of women and all Iraqis, regardless of religion or ethnicity. This hearing will explore some of the lessons learned from the experiences of other post-war nations and emerging democracies that have struggled to shape a constitution and rebuild legal institutions that promote principles of justice, freedom, and equality. I would like to briefly emphasize just a few points.

First, establishing security and the rule of law is an obligation of the United States under the Fourth Geneva Convention as an occupying power, and as our responsibility also to the people of Iraq, but I think it's extremely important to make clear that this hearing should not be construed as an attempt by the Senate or the U.S. Government to draft the next constitution of Iraq or reform its legal system. I believe that Senator Chafee's remarks were in that spirit.

The Iraqi people must decide their course. Drafting a constitution and reforming legal institutions must be a representative and consultative process, not a process imposed by the occupiers. It won't be easy, as past experiences with emerging democracies have shown, but it's absolutely necessary that this part of the effort succeed. The Iraqi people must be the authors of their own constitution and their own destiny.

Second, as we discuss the need for a revised Iraqi constitution, we should remember that the constitution, while important as a legal framework, is only one part of what must be a broader legal reform effort. Let's remember that Iraq actually had a constitution under Saddam Hussein, so in addition to redrafting Iraq's constitution, efforts must be made to rebuild institutions like the police, prisons, and the judiciary.

The Iraqi people also must consider what kind of mechanism they want to establish to account for and address past injustices by Saddam Hussein's regime. We should support Iraqis in developing just such a constitution, but also a functioning and reliable legal system to enforce it, or else we risk doing them a great disservice. I look forward to learning more about these issues from our witnesses today as well.

Finally, I recognize that the United States had great success in drafting the constitutions of post-World War II Japan and Germany, and we'll hear today from some experts about those experiences, but I believe it's important to note that some of our recent legal reform initiatives have been challenging, and have sometimes had mixed success. There is no one-size-fits-all approach to drafting a constitution or rebuilding a legal system in a post war country, and I hope the hearing this afternoon will explore some of the lessons learned from other legal reform efforts, from South Africa to East Timor.

We have a number of more recent examples of constitutional reform available to consider. We know that genuine consultation and civic participation are not easy to achieve, and that the most effective mechanisms for ensuring legitimacy are sometimes culturally and historically specific to a given society.

So I thank the two chairmen for convening this hearing, and I look forward to hearing from our witnesses.

Senator CORNYN. Thank you, Senator Feingold. I couldn't agree with you and Senator Chafee more about the way you characterize this challenge. We must help in every way possible to assist the Iraqis to establish the rule of law and a system of self-government. The challenge, though, comes in dealing with the basic security needs that are so obviously pressing upon us at this time, and to allow security to then give way to the constitution-making by the Iraqi people and then self-government under the rule of law. How we do that, how we assist without imposing ourselves I guess is the great challenge that confronts our Nation at this time.

I'd like to ask the members of the first panel to come up and have a seat at the witness table, and I will introduce them as they assume their places. Our first panel is comprised of experts who can speak both to the history of and the present situation in Iraq. Their testimony will be critical to understanding the needs and present conditions of the Iraqi people, and in drafting an Iraqi constitution that will actually work to preserve their freedoms.

First, we are pleased to have Dr. Kenneth Pollack on the panel. Dr. Pollack is a senior fellow in foreign policy studies at the Brookings Institution and director of research of the Saban Center for Middle East Policy at Brookings. During the Clinton administration, Dr. Pollack served in the National Security Council first as Director for Near East and South Asian Affairs, and later as Director for Persian Gulf Affairs. He is the author of *The Threatening Storm: The Case for Invading Iraq,* a book he published in 2002.

Professor Bernard Haykel is assistant professor of Middle Eastern studies and history at New York University. His academic career has focused on Islamic law and political and social history. In 2002, he published *Revival and Reform in Early Modern Islam.* He received a Ph.D. from Oxford University in Islamic studies in 1998.

Professor Khaled Abou El Fadl is the Omar and Esmeralda Alfi distinguished fellow in Islamic law at UCLA Law School. He was born in Kuwait, and grew up in Egypt and Kuwait. He is the author of numerous books on Islamic law, and has practiced law in both the United States and the Middle East. He received his Ph.D. in Islamic studies from Princeton in 1999, and has served on the UCLA law faculty since 1998.

Mr. Sermid Al-Sarraf is an Iraqi-American lawyer currently practicing in Los Angeles, California. He testifies today in his capacity as a member of the Iraqi Jurists' Association and the Working Group on Transitional Justice of the State Department's Future of Iraq project.

I notice that in his written remarks he quotes from a speech which I gave earlier this month at the American Enterprise Institute, so naturally I'm particularly interested in hearing his testimony today. That's very gracious of you.

Ms. Zainab Salbi is also a native of Iraq, and I must say, please accept my apologies if I mispronounce your name in any way. With a name like mine, I'm particularly sensitive to people mispronouncing your name, and I apologize.

She's the founder and president of Women for Women International, which matches U.S. women with foreign women in desperate circumstances. Over 40,000 people worldwide have been connected by Women for Women International. Now in eight countries, the organization has distributed more than $6 million in direct aid and micro-credit loans, and trained thousands of women in rights awareness.

So as you can see, we have a number of excellent panelists today on both the first and second panels. In order to ensure we have an opportunity to hear from each of them, and ensure we have ample time for members to ask questions, I will ask each witness to keep their opening statements to 5 minutes or less each. Of course, your longer written remarks will be submitted for the record so we will have an opportunity to understand all of your views in proper context.

I will take the opportunity to mention that without objection we will leave the record open until 5 p.m. next Wednesday, July 2, for members to submit additional documents into the record and for members to ask questions in writing of any of the panelists.

And with that, we will first hear from Dr. Pollack. Welcome.

STATEMENT OF KENNETH M. POLLACK, SENIOR FELLOW, SABAN CENTER FOR MIDDLE EAST POLICY, BROOKINGS INSTITUTION

Dr. POLLACK. Thank you very much, Mr. Chairman.

Mr. Chairman, these are extremely important hearings that you are holding. They are important because I think it's important to start by remembering our own history. The United States started off with a constitution that was called the Articles of Confederation. I think it's fair to say that the Articles of Confederation were not a very good constitution, and as a result, they led to paralysis, revolts, and could have provoked civil war, perhaps even a dissolution of this country, so it is from that lesson of our own country's history that we should keep in mind what may happen in Iraq.

Constitutions matter. They have a tremendous impact, a profound impact on the future of a country; and I think that it is fair to say that had the United States stuck with the Articles of Confederation, we almost certainly would not have lived to enjoy the strength and prosperity that we have today. Indeed, we might not still be a single Nation, had we lived under that constitution, and there are countless other examples throughout history.

Now, that said, the position of the United States with regard to Iraq's constitution is going to be a very delicate issue, as all of you have suggested in your opening remarks. In fact, I would suggest that the United States must walk a proverbial tightrope with regard to Iraq's constitution. On the one hand, the United States cannot dictate a constitution to the Iraqis. Iraqis must believe that this is their own constitution, reflective of their own values and their own traditions, and not one dictated by a foreign power.

But by the same token, Iraqis would not be the first country to get it wrong if left entirely to their own devices. As I've just mentioned, the United States got it wrong, and plenty of other countries have gotten it wrong over the course of time. Weimar, Germany is another that got it wrong with disastrous consequences. Iraq is too important a country and too important a part of the world for the rest of the world to simply take a hands-off approach and say to the Iraqis, we'll throw you in the water and see if you can sink or swim.

So the trick for the United States and for any other country out there in the world with an interest in seeing the success of a stable and prosperous new Iraqi society is to find ways to help guide the Iraqi constitutional progress without actually directing it. With this in mind, it's important to remember that we will be embarking on, in some ways, a new project. We will be helping the Iraqi people to create the first true Arab democracy.

Now, there have been examples of Arab democracies in the past. Lebanon is a particularly good example. But what the Iraqis seem to have in mind, what we certainly have in mind, and what others in the United Nations and elsewhere around the world seem to have in mind for Iraqis is something very different. It will be very important to allow Iraqis to determine what that new Arab Iraqi democracy looks like. We should keep in mind the examples of other countries around the world, Japan, Italy, so many other countries around the world which have democracies, but democracies that look very different from that of the United States. As someone said, we should keep in mind the broad parameters of democracy, and not so much the specifics.

With regard to Iraq, the goals for a constitution for Iraq should be broad, fairly basic. A constitution for Iraq should try to hold the country together by giving all of the members of Iraqi society a stake in the success of that new government, that new enterprise, and so therefore the values of fairness and egalitarianism have to be critical elements of any new Iraqi constitution.

In addition, because of Iraq's well-known ethnic, religious, tribal and other fractures, it will be critical that such a new constitution avoids the pitfall of a tyranny of the majority. This is another problem that we have seen throughout the history of democracies that can be particularly pernicious, especially in a situation like Iraq's, where so many members of the Iraqi community have been oppressed at various points in time by other members of the community. If the Iraqis believe that one group will be able to grab power and use the power of the central government to oppress the rest of the country, this constitution will be bound to fail.

And finally, a new constitution for Iraq must be one that creates incentives for compromise across the entire spectrum of Iraq. Too often in Iraqi history over the last 80 years, the system of government has fomented divisions, has encouraged the fissures already inherent in Iraqi society, pried them open rather than trying to help bring them together, and therefore creating these compromises will be critical.

How to do that? Again, I think the details need to be left to the Iraqis, but I think that some things can be pointed to. First, I think that Americans and others might suggest to the Iraqis that they look hard at the American system of government and the American Constitution. I say that not necessarily as an American chauvinist, because I think while our system worked for us, it may not have worked for others around the world, but in the case of Iraq, I think that there are real advantages to be found in the American system of government, advantages which would work well for the kinds of problems that the Iraqi people will have to overcome.

The focus on individual rights, on ensuring that the central government's powers are limited in terms of their ability to impose upon the individual are critical elements of our Constitution that would be extremely helpful in the Iraqi context.

A system of checks and balances is another extremely important issue, whereby the Iraqi people can become much more comfortable, much more confident in the system of government if it had a similar set of checks and balances to our own.

And finally, our system of geographic representation, which encourages compromise, as I've suggested before, which is critical. While it is true that the north is largely Kurdish-Sunni, while it is true that the south is a majority Shi'ah-Arab, and that the northwest of Iraq is a majority Sunni-Arab, so it is also true that there are very important areas of overlap inside Iraq, and a geographically based system would create mixed constituencies, the representatives of which would have inherent justifications for trying to reach compromise solutions, rather than trying to push things to extremes. These are the kinds of broad concepts that I think the United States and other countries with long histories of democracies could bring to the Iraqis as they try to frame their constitution, and suggest to them might be models, might be ways to think about crafting their own constitution that might be helpful in creating a constitution that can deliver a strong, stable, prosperous, and pluralist Iraq for the future. Thank you.

[The prepared statement of Dr. Pollack follows:]

Prepared Statement of Kenneth M. Pollack

BUILDING A DEMOCRATIC IRAQ

As the people of the United States of America learned over 200 years ago, building a stable, functional democracy isn't easy. Our own first effort, the Articles of Confederation, were a dismal failure that produced paralysis and rebellion. It is safe to say that had the government of the United States remained as constructed by that initial constitution, our nation would never have achieved the strength or the prosperity that it has today. Indeed, it is an open question whether we would even be a single nation today.

The example of the Articles of Confederation is an important lesson that the course of a nation will be shaped, even determined by its constitution. Machiavelli knew this and it is why he—a philosopher whose name is axiomatically associated with autocracy—believed that a vibrant Republic was the best form of government.

Thus, there is little doubt that if a pluralist form of government is to succeed in Iraq, the question of the specific composition of the state is critical. Especially given Iraq's well-known ethnic, religious and tribal fractures, building a state that can assuage popular fears and address the specific problems of the country will be essential to seal these divisions and produce a unified, peaceful and prosperous new Iraqi nation.

For better or worse, the United States must me part of this process. This will be a very difficult task. We must walk a proverbial tight-rope.

On the one hand, the more that the United States can leave the process of constituting a new Iraqi government to the Iraqi people themselves, the better for all involved. Iraqis are fiercely nationalistic. What's more, their unhappy experience with British colonialism creates the potential for heavy-handed U.S. involvement to resonate in a very negative manner, possibly sparking visceral resistance to what otherwise might be perfectly reasonable and even beneficial actions. Over the long term, the more that Iraqis believe that their constitution really is their constitution—written by Iraqis for Iraqis—the greater the likelihood that such a constitution will be accepted, respected, and obeyed.

On the other hand, it is just not clear that the Iraqi people know what is best for them yet. Certainly, Iraq does not have a history of good government which the average Iraqi might use as a reference point. Iraqis would not be the first people to devise a faulty new constitution because they simply had never done it before. Indeed, as I have already noted, the American people did the same, even though we had the helpful example of a reasonably benevolent and republican (for that era) government in England. Across the world, there are too many examples of failed new constitutions to list. In recent years, Bosnia is, example enough of how even the best intentioned people can set up a government but out of inexperience, make mistakes that can prove crippling politically, economically, and socially.

Thus, left to their own devices, the Iraqis may not make the best choices. But Iraq is too important a country in too important a part of the world for the United States to simply "throw them in the water and see if they can swim." In addition, because of the rather severe divisions among the Iraqi people, if a new Iraqi constitution proved as unworkable as the Articles of Confederation, to continue with that example, it could quickly produce a slide into chaos, secession, and civil war. The United States arid the international community could not abide that, nor should we contribute to a process by which the Iraqi people are likely to suffer another tragedy having endured 34 years of Ba'athist tyranny already.

The trick will be for the United States to guide the presence without directing it. Here, the role of the United Nations and other international institutions could be extremely helpful if only because Iraqis do not suspect the UN of colonial ambitions. So too might other allies prove helpful. The Scandinavians are widely seen as sympathetic, humanitarian and disinterested, for example, and they might be able to help guide the Iraqis in ways that Washington cannot directly. Other non-Western democracies might also play useful roles. So too might a country like Bangladesh, which has enjoyed a reasonable progress on the path toward democracy without losing its Islamic identity.

Islam and Democracy

The example of Bangladesh raises an important issue with regard to Iraq: the question of Islam and Democracy. There is simply no reason that the Islamic character of a country should prevent it from adopting a democratic system of government. Bangladesh is proof of that. In Turkey, over the past few months, we have seen stunning changes in which an Islamist party is bringing true democracy—sure proof that Islam and democracy are not mutually exclusive.

Islam is one of the world's great religions. One that is meant to be meaningful for all time and in all places. As such, while it does contain numerous injunctions as to how believers are to live their lives—what they should and should not do—there is nothing to suggest that the religion of Islam is compatible with only one form of governance. (As an aside, given the early, egalitarian and consociational method of rule employed by the first leaders of the Islamic state, an argument can be made that Islam is more compatible with democracy than autocracy).

Islam is a religion of infinite variety. There is not only the well-known Sunni-Shi 'ite split, but also varying schools of jurispnidence within each, a range of Sufi sects, and numerous regional varieties. Indeed, Clifford Geertz, the great Western scholar of Islam, has observed that Islam in Morocco (the western end of the Islamic world) and Islam in Indonesia (the eastern end of the Islamic world) are very different religions, heavily influenced by the cultural traditions of each nation and more like them than each other. In Iran, the Ayatollah Khomeini had to develop a completely new doctrine—the notion of velayat-e faqih or rule by the jurisprudent—one completely at odds with traditional Shi'ite beliefs, to justify his rule over the Iranian state.

While this is clearly an extreme example—certainly not one the United States should encourage Iraq to emulate, it does make clear that Islam is neither fixed nor immutable. Indeed, this "Orientalist" interpretation of Islam has long since been discredited and should not be allowed to creep back into real world considerations of the future of Iraq which hold such importance for the Iraqi people and the entire world.

An Iraqi Democracy

If it is important to remember that Islam is not a "one-note" religion, so too is it important to remember that the same is true of democracy. When we speak of democracy, too often we allow our own cultural or individual associations to obscure the meaning of the word. Democracy is rule by the people. In practical terms, it means a political system in which the actions of the government reflect the will of the people, in which those actions are transparent to the population, and the officials charged with executing its policies are accountable to the people. While it is hard to imagine a truly democratic system without elections, elections are not synonymous with democracy. They are just one element of it and not necessarily the defining element.

Many governments around the world have met these conditions while adopting very different models of democracy. Japan, Italy, and the United States are all democracies yet the workings of their political processes are as different as they are similar.

It will be important to keep this in mind when fostering the process of democracy in Iraq. We should think in broad terms. One of the great challenges for an Iraqi democracy is that it will be the first real Arab democracy. Thus one of the challenges will be helping Arab Iraqis develop a democratic system that is suited to their Arab culture just as Japanese democracy is harmonious with Japanese culture and Italian democracy is attuned to Italian culture.

(Indeed, this is where the success of democracy in Iraq could have important ramifications in the Middle East beyond Iraq. Part of the problem with current efforts to democratize the Arab world is that the Arabs have never seen a nation that was both truly democratic and Arab. But just as the success of Japanese democracy made it possible for other East Asians to imagine what democracy might look like in their country, so too might an Iraqi democracy allow other Arabs to understand and desire the same for their countries.)

Ultimately, building democracy in Iraq is not going to be easy. In particular there is the real possibility that Iraq's considerable problems would pervert elections, freedom of speech, or other democratic building blocks and produce illiberal results. Since the fall of the Ottoman Empire, Iraq has been badly governed. In large measure this is because of Iraq's well-known cleavages, and because the Iraqis are famously ungovernable—and had a wide reputation for such even under the Ottomans. This is why Iraq's experiences after independence were so unhappy, and why it took the bloodthirsty tyranny of Saddam Hussein to impose a terrible order on the country. These very features of Iraqi society that make it so hard to govern also demand a democratic system capable of dealing with its serious internal contradictions.

The greatest internal problem for democracy is the potential for one group, particularly Iraq's majority Shi'ah community, to dominate the country. Iraq's Shi'ah community, which comprises over 60 percent of the total population, might use free elections to transform its current exclusion from power to one of total dominance—and knowing this, Sunni Arabs, and perhaps the Kurds, might attempt to preemptively subvert a majority rule-based system. Thus the key for an Iraqi democracy will be to fashion a system that addresses the potential problem of a "tyranny of the majority."

A parliamentary form of democracy would probably be inappropriate for Iraq's political needs because it would exacerbate these problems. A parliamentary form of government—in which the majority party controls both the executive and legislative branches—would reinforce the tyranny of the majority, terrify Iraq's minorities, and probably cause them to try to undermine or circumvent the system to protect themselves from the authority of the central government. Worst of all would be a parliamentary system of proportional representation, which would simply reinforce identification and affiliation along these sectarian lines. Proportional representation in Iraq would harden Iraq's Kurds to vote as Kurds, its Shi'ah to vote as Shi'ah and its Sunni Arabs to vote as Sunni Arabs with no deviation or room for middle ground positions.

Nevertheless, it is possible to envision a form of democracy that should be able to cope with Iraq's political problems. Perhaps surprisingly, a democratic system with some similarities to the American system would appear to best fit the bill. Iraq needs a democratic system that ensures minority rights, limits the ability of the central government to impose its will on its citizens, includes checks and balances to ensure that control of one part of the government does not translate into a form of dictatorship of the majority, and encourages compromise and cooperation among members of otherwise well-defined groupings. Features of Iraq's democracy should include:

Defining the rights of every individual and limiting the trespasses of the central government;

Declaring that all powers not reserved to the federal government are instead vested in local governments to further limit central government authorities. In particular, rights to language and religious expression should be expressly noted;

Creating a further series of checks and balances within the federal system to limit the powers of the government and particularly the ability of any group to employ the power of the central government to repress other members of Iraqi society;

Electing a President indirectly, in order to ensure that different communities have a say in who is chosen. in particular, Iraq should look to other systems (like that of Malaysia) that work to ensure that candidates are acceptable to multiple constituencies and are not simply imposed by the largest group on the rest of the country; and

Employing a system of representation in the legislature that is determined by geography—not pure party affiliation as in many parliamentary systems—to encourage cooperation across ethnic and religious lines.

This last point is an important one in thinking about Iraqi democracy. Although there is a fair degree of communal correlation with geography (i.e., the Kurds live in the north, the Shi'ah in the south, and the Sunnis in the west) there are also important regions of overlap. In Baghdad, and large chunks of central Iraq, Sunni, Shi'ah, and Kurds are well mixed. By insisting on a system of geographically determined representation, Iraqi legislators elected from these mixed districts would have an incentive to find compromise solutions to national problems to try to please their mixed constituencies. This will be crucial to the success of an Iraqi democracy because it is vital to create a constituency for compromise within the Iraqi central government.

Indeed, this points out one of the great problems of a parliamentary system (particularly proportional representation) for Iraq, because by emphasizing party membership in determining legislative elections, the legislators themselves have less incentive to try to reach compromises across party lines and much more incentive to slavishly follow party ideology. It is a system that tends to push legislators to extremes. What is needed in Iraq is a system that instead encourages them to move toward the center and reach compromises. The American system has become almost infamous for this tendency, so much so that on election day it is often impossible to tell the candidates apart because they all cling so desperately to the middle ground.

One technique that might be applicable in Iraq would be to require candidates to receive a certain percentage of votes from different communities. Thus, a legislator from Kirkuk (a mixed Sunni Arab and Kurdish area) would be required to receive at least one third of the votes of both the Arab and Kurdish communities. In such a system, a demagogue or sectarian extremist would be unlikely to garner sufficient backing to win, while moderates and those amenable to compromise would. This approach could be applied at other levels as well. For example, a candidate for Chief Executive would have to receive a similar percentage from different communities, again discouraging chauvinism.

No Other Alternatives

Building a democracy in Iraq is not going to be quick or easy, nor is there any guarantee that the effort will succeed. However, it is a necessary course for the United States, the international community, and the people of Iraq to follow. I speak not as an expert on democracy, nor as an advocate for democratic systems, but purely as a specialist on Iraqi affairs. Although there can be no guarantee that democracy will succeed in Iraq, I think it a near certainty that any other system of government will fail there.

The problems of Iraq are so great that any other system is bound to fail. Indeed, the history of Iraq is that they all have failed. Monarchy, oligarchy, and autocracy have all failed to produced stability, prosperity, and tranquility. Both the monarchy and the savage brutality of Saddam's reign produced stability without prosperity or tranquility. The pre-Saddam revolving dictatorships produced none of these ends. In the future, any resort to these or other approaches—theocracy, tribal rule, consociational oligarchy—would doubtless produce more of the same. If the United States and our international partners are not going to see Iraq slip into chaos and civil war, we are going to have to ensure that the Iraqis are able to build a stable democracy. That could be very difficult, but it is also not impossible.

Senator CORNYN. Thank you, Dr. Pollack.

Professor Haykel.

STATEMENT OF BERNARD HAYKEL, PROFESSOR, DEPARTMENT OF MIDDLE EASTERN STUDIES, NEW YORK UNIVERSITY

Dr. HAYKEL. Thank you, Mr. Chairman. I would like to submit the statement for the record, and I will summarize it here in a set of points, keeping them brief, and keeping the overlap with my colleague to a minimum.

Clearly, the process that the United States has embarked on is complicated and fraught with great difficulties. The difficulties have to do with the nature of Iraqi society, its violent past, its authoritarian past as well, in addition to the regional pressures that countries around Iraq are exerting.

The U.S., in redevising or recreating this constitution, should pursue a proscriptive rather than prescriptive role, or policy. This is a fancy way of basically saying that we should just establish the broad parameters of what this constitution has to look like, or ought to look like—it should be democratic, it should be pluralist—but we should not get into the details of what this constitution will involve. This is for the Iraqis to do.

One thing that should be borne in mind is that Iraqis, whether exiles or Iraqis who have stayed in Iraq throughout this period, are an extremely talented group of people. They are very, very well-educated. The jurists both outside and inside are extremely talented, and it should be left to them to make these kinds of decisions.

Now, I have surveyed the various proposals that the different groups have made or offered so far, and all seem to favor a federal structure for Iraq, and the advantage of that—and if they wish to keep the federal structure, we should by all means support this, and it seems to be going and headed in that direction, and the advantage of that is that it would accommodate the three major groups that constitute the Iraqi population, and will prevent any one of the groups from taking over or dominating the others.

These three groups—the Sunni Kurds, the Sunni Arabs, and the Shiite Arabs—are really the major groups that form the Iraqi population and will have to come to an accommodation with each other over the form of rule that Iraq will have.

The one crucial thing that the United States should not, again in establishing this parameter, should not insist on is that the constitution of Iraq should not have specific roles for these various groups embedded in the constitution. The example of Lebanon is extremely crucial to bear in mind here. In Lebanon, the constitution as set up has the various confessions in the country playing set roles politically. What this means is that it cements the differences along sectarian religious lines, it prevents groups from creating alliances across these sectarian religious lines, and it prevents a genuine sense of nationalism and citizenry from being formed.

So this is another thing to bear in mind, and it seems to me, like Dr. Pollack said, one good way in which Iraqis can create alliances across the religious divide is to have the districts that are formed in Iraq to be based on territorial considerations, rather than religious or ethnic considerations. In other words, geography, demography, economic viability should be the bases for the division of Iraq, for the constituent units of Iraq, rather than religion or ethnic identity.

In this regard, I think the United States should, as soon as possible, establish a census for the population of Iraq, so that we have a baseline to know exactly what the Iraqi population looks like in ethnic, religious, linguistic, socioeconomic terms.

I would like to raise now the issue of Islam. One unifying factor for the Iraqi population is Islam. Ninety-five percent of all Iraqis are Muslim, and they clearly want Islam to play a role in whatever constitutional setup they decide on. This should be something that the United States should encourage, and not discourage. If Islam is given a role at a symbolic level where, let's say, one article of the constitution states that Islam is the official religion of the State of Iraq, this should be perfectly acceptable to us.

Many countries in the Muslim and Arab world have this. Malaysia is one, Yemen is one, and there is no threat from giving Islam this symbolic role. There is no threat of a theocracy emerging if Islam is given symbolic representation in the constitution.

Iraq is not likely to turn into a theocracy, either Shiite or Sunni, because of the way the population is broken up and because of its history. I don't want to go into the details. My statement states why this is the case. We should not fear a theocracy emerging in Iraq at all. It would not work, and the Iraqis themselves don't seem to want it. The majority of Iraqis don't seem to want it.

The other issue that we should bear in mind is: whatever we do in Iraq has wider policy implications in the Middle East; what we do there is crucially important because Arabs at the moment are looking at us, and there is an equivalency being established between our occupation in the country and what the Israelis are doing to the Palestinians.

This is how Arabs outside Iraq seem to be making this sort of equation between our role and the Israeli role, and this is a very bad thing. We should break that linkage as quickly and as effectively, as efficiently as possible, and our allowing Islam to play a role in the constitution framework of Iraq is one way of doing that.

If Arab Muslims see that the United States is not against Islam but is allowing Iraqis to express their Islamic identity, this would again play a very important role in our fight against people like the bin Laden, who are arguing that the United States is at war with Islam.

There are secular forces in Iraq as well, and we should let them play a role, but not overemphasize the role that they will be playing, nor underemphasize it. Religion will certainly have a role to play in the constitution, and I think we should look favorably upon that.

Finally, Iraq did have a period of political pluralism, which was limited under the Hashimite monarchy. They did write a constitution in 1925, which was not a bad model, actually, to base oneself on for this constitution, the forthcoming constitution.

I think it's important for us, that is, for the United States, to invoke and revise that period in Iraqi history. At the very least, it will make our efforts seem more legitimate against this historical backdrop and also make the efforts that we're engaged in seem less contrived and artificial.

If I may, just one last, last point. The United States at the moment is engaged in a process of de-Ba'athification in Iraq. I've calculated the numbers of Ba'athists who will be excluded from all offices. It comes to somewhere around 220,000 people. Now, these 220,000 individuals have families that depend on them. A very conservative estimate would mean that at least 1 million Iraqis would be out of jobs, maybe even up to 5 million Iraqis. That's 20 percent of the population. I think we ought to reconsider also our policy of de-Ba'athification to make the number of people in the Ba'ath who are excluded from office the smallest and lowest number possible in order not to exclude such a large number of people from State office.

Thank you very much.

[The prepared statement of Dr. Haykel follows:]

PREPARED STATEMENT OF BERNARD HAYKEL

The process of establishing a constitution for Iraq is complicated and fraught with difficulties. This is because of the divided and fractious nature of Iraqi society, its violent and authoritarian past and regional pressures exerted by neighboring countries. The process the United States has embarked on in rebuilding Iraq is unprecedented in the region and there is no model from the Arab or Islamic worlds that can be emulated. In what follows, I will present some of the broad guidelines that should inform the policy of the United States in this process.

The U.S. should pursue a proscriptive rather than a prescriptive policy. In other words, we should delineate the parameters within which the constitution should be formulated and not dictate the specific details of the Iraqi constitution. The U.S., for example, must insist that Iraq be a democratic country, but it should not delve into such detailed issues as to whether the form of governance ought to be federal or unitary or the executive be presidential or parliamentarian. Such questions should be resolved by the Iraqis themselves in a constitutional convention. Iraq has a very talented pool of individuals (jurists, academics and politicians), among the exiles and those who never left Iraq, and delineating the specifics of the constitution should devolve on them as they will be responsible ultimately for its success as well as its failure.

The various political groups that are now competing for a say in the future of Iraq are advocating a federal structure, one that would accommodate, in particular, the non-Arab Kurds (approximately 20% of the population), but also the Shiite Arabs (approx. 60% of the population) in the south and the Sunni Arabs (approx. 20% of the population). Federalism is an appealing formula because it would prevent one group dominating the others, a real prospect given Iraq's history and demographic realities. A constitutional parameter that must be established by the United States is that no one of the three dominant groups should be allowed to dominate the others, as the Sunni Arabs have done until the defeat of Saddam Hussein's regime. By the same token, however, the United States must endeavor to prevent the constitution from enshrining Iraqi politics along ethnic (Kurd vs. Arab) and/or confessional (Sunni vs. Shiite) lines. The example of Lebanon is important to keep in mind in this regard. Here the constitutional setup cements confessional rule, and this has prevented the emergence of secular political formations and allegiances that cut across religious divides. As a result, Lebanese nationalism and institutions have remained weak and all politics is confessional—a sure recipe for future strife. Clearly there is a tension between establishing a power sharing arrangement among the three major groups in Iraq and allowing the system to function and evolve on a non-ethnic and non-confessional basis. There is no ready formula for resolving this tension but below are some ideas about how one can think about accomplishing this.

There are a number of ways to mitigate the political effects of the ethnic and confessional divisions in Iraq. The first is to prevent the electoral districts from being drawn purely on the basis of ethnic/confessional lines. The country should ideally be divided in accordance with territorial considerations (geography, demography, economic viability) and not ethnic or confessional ones. This would amalgamate different groups of Iraqis together, forcing them to make compromises and allegiances that cut across their divisions. Despite the commonly accepted tri-partite division of Iraq into a Shi'i south, a Sunni Arab middle and west and a Kurdish north, the country's population is more mixed ethnically and in terms of religion. Therefore, it would be possible to create some constituent units that have a mixed population. In this regard, it would prove beneficial for all the parties concerned, the United States as well as the Iraqis, to organize a population census in order to obtain a real sense of the demographics.

Another unifying factor in Iraq is Islam, the religion of some 95% of all Iraqis. All the emerging signals from the Iraqis appear to indicate that they wish Islam to play a role in the future political framework of the country. The United States should not prevent this, especially if reference to Islam remains at the symbolic level such as an article in the constitution declaring Islam to be the official religion of Iraq or another that states that the Shari'a (i.e., Islamic law) is a source of law in the country. Both Malaysia and Yemen are good examples of countries in which Islam is accorded this symbolic role and yet both remain firmly anti-theocratic. The U.S. should not fret about Iraq becoming a theocracy in the Iranian or Saudi mold—this is not going to happen. Except for a minority, the Shi'is of Iraq do not think of Iran as a model to be emulated, and more importantly they could never realistically impose such a model on the remaining Sunni population. Furthermore, the Shi'is of Iraq have a different history from those in Iran: in social and political terms they are organized differently and their clerics have traditionally competed with those in Qom in Iran. In addition, some of the dominant figures among the Iraqi Shi'is (e.g., Ayatollah Sistani) are arguing for a quietist position, one in which the clerics remain formally outside all political institutions.

As in the case of the Shi'is, the Sunnis of Iraq cannot impose a Sunni Islamist regime on the majority Shi'is. The Sunnis are divided ethnically and are demographically in the minority. More importantly, and unlike the Iranian-backed Shi'is, the Sunni islamists have no ideological framework for ruling the country other than an ill-defined system of theocratic despotism. Only recently have Sunni Islamists (e.g., Muslim Brothers, Wahhabi-Salafis) emerged on the Iraqi political scene, and as such they remain an unknown quantity, except for al-Qaeda. Those who advocate violence must be fought militarily, whereas those who agree to participate through the peaceful means of electoral politics should be permitted to compete in the political process. The United States should proscribe all forms of theocratic rule, be it Sunni or Shi'i, but we should not deny Iraqis the desire to make appeal to Islam at the level of political symbolism and as a vague guideline for a just order. Permitting this will serve an important foreign policy goal.

We should bear in mind that the U.S. project of rebuilding a democratic Iraq is being undertaken in the context of our wider policy aims in the Arab and Muslim worlds. This endeavor is being closely monitored by the Arabs in the region, many of whom are arguing for seeing an equivalence between the Israeli occupation in the Palestinian territories and the U.S. occupation of Iraq. We must attempt to break this linkage whenever possible. Allowing Iraqis to make appeal to Islam in their constitution is one way of doing this, because it undermines Osama Bin Laden's false claim that the United States is at war with Islam.

It is important to bear in mind that there are secular political forces in Iraq and these should neither be sidelined nor for that matter be unduly privileged. The Kurds, for instance, are represented by secular parties and many of the Iraqi exiles are secular. Furthermore, the dominant ideology of Iraq since the early 1960s, the Ba'ath, had been nationalist and secular in orientation and this is bound to have left some impression on the political consciousness of the Iraqi people. It remains to be seen what weight the secularist forces will have in the country once matters have settled down further. Nonetheless, it is unlikely that any radical secular program will take hold in Iraq. A majority of Muslim Iraqis will not agree to abandon the Shari'a in matters relating to personal status law (i.e., marriage, divorce, inheritance). Nor will non-Muslim Iraqis (Assyrians, Chaldeans, Armenians) abandon their religious courts in the same areas of the law. Religion therefore will remain a political factor, hopefully one relegated to the personal or private realm; a feature that should not prove unfamiliar to us in the United States.

Finally, Iraq has had a period of political pluralism (albeit limited) under the Hashimite monarchy—during which a constitution was written, in 1925. This document as well as the historical memories and practices of the pre-Ba'ath period must be invoked and revived at the present moment. At the very least, this would give the efforts of the United States a legitimizing historical backdrop and would make the attempt of reforming and rebuilding Iraq appear less contrived.

Senator CORNYN. Thank you, Professor.
Dr. El Fadl.

STATEMENT OF KHALED ABOU EL FADL, PROFESSOR OF LAW, UCLA SCHOOL OF LAW

Dr. EL FADL. Thank you very much. I'll start out by a comment about the nature of constitutions. I think it is important, as we go about playing the supportive role vis-a-vis Iraq, to remember that constitutions are documents that memorialize structural and procedural commitments, but that also, and even more importantly, constitutions are instruments for making ethical and moral commitments.

In that sense, it is important to remember that a constitution must reflect prevailing normativities, prevailing ethical and moral commitments within a social structure. But they also must be instruments capable of educating and sponsoring an evolving dialog within society. Constitutions that are static, that are closed the minute they are drafted, have an awfully terrible habit of failing.

Now, I think that it is crucial from the start that there be no dilution and no wavering on the ethical commitment made toward one significant moral issue, that is the issue of individual rights. I think that needs an honest and committed discourse, and one in which individual rights become the centerpoint and the core for a constitutionalism that would start the process of evolution and education in Iraq.

A constitution in Iraq will fail if the constitutional document, instead of being an expression of the moral commitments of the Iraqi people, becomes a symbol of denial of sociopolitical autonomy. If the constitution is associated with such a denial, it will be, like many other constitutions in the Middle East propagated by an elite—whether the elite is pro-Western or anti-Western, it hardly makes a difference. They become only paper and largely irrelevant and marginal to what happens in society.

The second situation where a constitution in Iraq will fail, is if the constitution becomes a symbol for losing religious authenticity, or what the Iraqis might consider as a religious truth. Here, it is important to remember that contrary to popular understandings or stereotypes, the Ba'ath regime, the regime of Saddam Hussein, one of the ways that it has traumatized the Iraqi people is by excluding the possibility of free, authentic, and genuine religious expression in Iraq.

The regime of Saddam, or the Ba'ath party, which was partially secular, narrowly defined legitimate religion and severely restricted what religious manifestations might take place in society. Therefore, we should not be alarmed or threatened or go into some sort of Doomsday scenario if Iraqis, as a reaction to that trauma of suppressing their religiosity, wish in the form of a constitution to make some type of affirmation of their religiosity, and of their religious commitments.

In fact, I agree with Bernard Haykel that we should welcome that and see it as a positive thing. As a matter of foreign policy it can only work to our advantage, as long as whatever commitments are made vis-a-vis Islam are made in light of the commitments made vis-a-vis individual human rights.

Thank you.

[The prepared statement of Dr. El Fadl follows:]

PREPARED STATEMENT OF KHALED ABOU EL FADL

Introduction to Islamic Concepts of the State

The relationship of Islam to the state, both in theory and practice, has been complex and multifaceted. Islam, as a system of beliefs embodying a multitude of moral and ethical principles, has inspired a wide range of social and political practices, and a diverse set of legal interpretations and determinations known collectively as the Shari'a. Muslims believe the Shari'a to be divine law, in the sense that the Shari'a is based on the human interpretations and extrapolations upon the revealed holy book, the Qur'an, and the authentic precedents of the Prophet, known as the Sunna. Therefore, the Shari'a (which literally means the way to God or the fountain and spring source of goodness) is the sum total of the various efforts of Muslim scholars to interpret and search for the Divine Will as derived from the Qur'an and Sunna. Importantly, through the course of fourteen centuries, Muslim scholars emphasized that the main objective of Shari'a law is to serve the interests and well being, as well as protect the honor and dignity, of human beings. There is no single code of law or particular set of positive commandments that represent Shari'a law. Rather, Shari'a law is constituted of several schools of jurisprudential thought that are considered equally orthodox and authoritative. In the Sunni world there are four dominant schools of thought: the Shafi'is, Hanafis, Malikis and Hanbalis. In the Shi'i world, the dominant schools are the Ja'faris and Zaydis. The Sunni population of Iraq is predominately Hanafi, while the Shi'i population is predominantly Ja'fari.

The Historical Background of Muslim States

The first Muslim polity was the city-state led by the Prophet Muhammad in Medina. But after the Prophet Muhammad died, no human being or institution was deemed to inherit his legislative, executive, or moral power. In Islamic theology, there is no church or priestly class that is empowered to speak for God or represent His Will. There is a class of Shari'a specialists (jurists) known as the 'ulama' or 'fuqaha', who are distinguished by virtue of their learning and scholarship, but there is no formal procedure for ordination or investiture. These jurists are not thought to embody the Divine Will nor treated as the exclusive representatives of God's law. The authoritativeness that a particular jurist might enjoy is a function of his formal and informal education, and his social and scholastic popularity. As to their political and institutional role, in classical Islamic theory, jurists are supposed to play an advisory and consultative role, and to assume judicial positions in the administration of justice. It is an interesting historical fact that until the modern age, jurists never assumed direct political power. Although, historically, the jurists played important social and civil roles and often served as judges implementing Shari'a law and executive ordinances, for the most part, government in Islam remained secular. Until the modern age, a theocratic system of government in which a church or clergy rule in God's name was virtually unknown in Islam. Institutionally, Islam does not dictate a particular system of government, and in theory, there is no inconsistency or fundamental clash between Islam and democracy. The Qur'an dictates only that governance ought not be autocratic, and that the affairs of government should be conducted through consultation (shura). According to the classical jurisprudential theory, governance should be pursuant to a civil contract ('aqd) between the governor and the governed, and the ruler should obtain a pledge of support (bay'a) from the influential members of society as well as the majority of his constituency. In theory, rulers are supposed to consult with jurists, as well as other representative elements in society, and then, after concluding the consultative process, act upon the best interests of the people. In classical Islam, the consultative body was known as ahl al-hal wa al-aqd, and this body was supposed to be representative to the extent that it included the authoritative and popular jurists, and other influential members of society. There is substantial disagreement in the classical sources, however, on whether upon concluding the consultative process, the ruler is duty bound to adhere to the judgment of the majority, or whether he may act upon his own discretion, even if his opinion is contrary to the view expressed by the majority. This doctrine was known as ilzamiyyat al-shura. There was a strong consensus among the classical scholars that in principle, consultation itself is mandatory, but they disagreed on the extent to which a ruler is free to act in contradiction to the will of the majority as expressed in the consultative process.

Outside this basic framework, the state was supposed to respect Shari'a, and strive to fulfill Shari'a's ultimate objectives in society. Historically, the prevailing form of government in Islam was known as the Caliphate, which in reality was dynastic and authoritarian. For about thirty years after the death of the Prophet, Muslims succeeded in establishing a form of government with a strong democratic orientation, but upon the rise of the Umayyad Dynasty, the democratic experiment came to an end, and power became concentrated in the hands of particular families or military forces. In pre-modern practice, to the extent that rulers adhered to the process of consultation at all, the consultative body was usually not representative of the governed, and membership in such a body was typically the product of political patronage and not the outcome of a democratic elective process.

The Adoption of European Laws by Muslim Countries in the Modern Age

In the post-Colonial era, after most Muslim nation states achieved independence, the relationship between Islam and the state gained a new sense of urgency. At issue were the extent to which Shari'a law would play a role in the legal systems of the new-found nation-states, and the extent to which Islam would play a role in affairs of governance. In the period between the 1940's and 1960's, most Muslim countries opted for a nationalist, republican, secular model in which there is a very strong executive power, supported by weaker legislative and judicial branches of government. Some countries, such as Saudi Arabia, continued to be governed by a strong royal family, a consultative branch of limited powers, and a judiciary that implemented a mixture of customary law and Shari'a-based law. Most Muslim countries, such as Egypt, Iraq, and Kuwait imported the French Civil and Criminal Codes, and organized their legal systems according to the Civil Law legal tradition. A few countries such as Pakistan, Indonesia, and Malaysia were influenced by the British Common Law system, which they supplemented by various statutory laws enacted in specific fields. The extent to which the Islamic legal tradition was integrated into modern legal systems varied widely from one country to another, and also varied in accordance with the particular field of law in question. More specifically, in commercial and civil legal matters, most Muslim countries generated a synchronistic system, which was predominantly French, Swiss, or British, amended by various concepts and doctrines inspired by the Islamic legal tradition. In criminal matters, most countries adopted the French or British systems of criminal justice. Countries such as Saudi Arabia and post-revolutionary Iran rejected Western influences, and claimed to base their criminal laws on the Islamic tradition. Most of the countries of the Arabian Peninsula, some African nations, and Iran continued to adhere to the Islamic tradition in matters of personal injury and tort law. This was manifested primarily by the incorporation of blood money (diya), and strict caps on financial liability in cases of personal injury. Personal and family law remained the field most susceptible to Islamic influence. Most Muslim countries created courts of separate jurisdiction to handle matters related to inheritance, divorce, and marriage. In these fields, judges typically implement statutory laws, which were enacted as codifications of Islamic laws.

The Iraqi Legal Experience in the Modern Age

It is often said that Iraq was the cradle of civilization. This is definitely true as far as Iraq's long and rich jurisprudential experience. Before Saddam came to power, Iraq, in addition to Egypt, was one of the most influential countries in the development of the legal institutions and substantive laws of the Arabic speaking world. This was in part due to the high level of education enjoyed by the Iraqi elite, and the rich cultural experiences and cosmopolitan nature of Iraqi urban centers, such as Baghdad and Basra. Geographically, Iraq was at the central point where Arab, Persian, Kurdish, and Turkish cultures meet and interact. As noted above, Iraq was also home to both Shi'i and Sunni major centers of religious study. The rich and diverse makeup of Iraqi society itself allowed Iraq to be the beneficiary of ethnic, linguistic, religious, and sectarian cultural exchanges. This in turn was reflected in the fact that Iraqi legal thought was characterized by a distinctive synchronistic quality, open-mindedness, and a lack of xenophobic nativism.

Historically, the urban centers of Iraq, Baghdad, Basra, and Kufa, played central roles in the birth of Islamic jurisprudence, and they continued, over the span of a thousand years, to play a leading role in the development and evolution of the institutions and doctrines of Islamic law. In fact, the Hanafi and Ja'fari schools of Islamic jurisprudence, in particular, developed primarily in Kufa, Basra, and Baghdad in the first few centuries of Islam. Furthermore, Baghdad was the capital of the Abbasid Empire, the second major dynasty in Islam. As such, Iraq's intellectual heritage, especially as it relates to Islam's divine law, continued to carry considerable moral weight within the Muslim world.

After gaining independence from Britain in 1930, like most Arab countries, Iraq eventually adopted Civil Law and Criminal Law Codes, which were adapted from the French and Germanic legal systems. Iraq's personal law, however, continued to be based primarily on Islamic law. Like most Muslim countries, the continuing tension, and at times conflict, were between Iraq's Islamic legal heritage, and the legal system borrowed from Europe at the end of the Colonial era. Many aspects of the classical tradition of Islamic law conflicted with the newly adopted European-based Civil and Criminal laws, and as in the case of many other Muslim countries, there were considerable sociopolitical pressures, both internal and external, to simultaneously Islamize and modernize.

In the 1950's Iraq was at the forefront of the creative and demanding effort to adopt a system of law that was efficient, modern, and at the same time, Islamically legitimate. In this regard, the Iraqi Civil Code of 1953 was one of the most innovative and meticulously systematic codes of the Middle East. Iraqi jurists, working with the assistance of the famous Egyptian jurist Al-Sarihuri, drafted a code that balanced and merged elements of Islamic and French law in one of the most successful attempts to preserve the best of both legal systems. Furthermore, in 1959 Iraq promulgated the Code of Personal Status, which on the issues of family and testamentary law was at the time the most progressive Muslim code of law. Importantly, this Code merged elements of Sunni and Shi'i law to grant women greater rights as to marriage, divorce, and inheritance.

The Iraqi Ba'ath, a staunchly nationalist and secular party, came to power in 1968, and Saddam formally ascended to the presidency in 1979. It is fair to say that especially after Saddam rose to power, all creative and inspiring legal activity came to an end. Since coming to power, Saddam involved Iraq in a series of wars that enabled him to declare a constant state of national emergency and to rule mostly by executive order. The centralization of power in the hands of the Ba'ath and Saddam meant that legal institutions lost all vestiges of independence, and civil society became thoroughly co-opted by the ruling party. Increasingly, Iraqi law could no longer be described as either Islamic or French, but as distinctly and uniquely Saddamian. The death sentence was prescribed for a large variety of offenses including usurpation of public money, corruption, insulting the Presidency, and treason, which was defined very widely. The implementation of these laws was highly whimsical and largely contingent on the will of the party and President. Even foreign investments became largely dependent on having the proper connections to the ruling elite, and tapping into a network of businessmen who were sanctioned and protected by a clique that was close to Saddam and his family.

The Islamization of Laws in Modern Muslim Countries

The period between the 1960's and 1970's witnessed the emergence of fundamentalist Islamic movements that materially impacted the constitutional place of Islam in the various Muslim states. Building upon the positions of some pre-modern theological orientations, most fundamentalist groups, but not all, contended that sovereignty belongs only to God (al-hakimiyya li'llah), that governments ought to represent and give effect to the Divine Will, and that there ought to be a strict adherence to the detailed determinations of religious scholars. The fundamentalist orientations of that period are most accurately understood as oppositional nationalistic movements dissatisfied with the status quo, and utilizing religious symbolisms as a means of claiming authenticity and legitimacy. The problem, however, is that fundamentalists tended to treat Shari'a as a code of law containing unitary and uncontested specific legal determinations, and also tended to ignore the highly contextual socio-historical nature of most of Islamic jurisprudence. The Islamic legal tradition is too diverse, diffuse, and amorphous to yield to the type of narrow treatment afforded to it by fundamentalists. In addition, taken out of its socio-historical context, parts of Islamic legal tradition become problematic in terms of contemporary international human rights standards.

Although fundamentalist movements did not achieve direct power in most Muslim countries, they generated political pressure towards what might be described as greater symbolic Islamization. As a part of their Islamization efforts, a large number of Muslim countries drafted in their constitutions articles that either stated: "Shari'a is *the* main source of legislation," or "Shari'a law is *a* main source of legislation." The former version made Islamic law the near exclusive source of law for the nation, while the latter version mandated that Islamic law be only one of the several sources of law making in the country. Importantly, however, especially for countries that adopted the former version, the Shari'a clause was deemed not to be self-executing. This meant that the Shari'a clause was deemed to be addressed to the legislative and executive powers in the country, and not the judiciary. Accordingly, the judiciary would not, on its own initiative, give effect to Islamic law. Rather, Shari'a law needed to be implemented or executed by statutory law, and only upon the enactment of such statutory laws would the judiciary be bound to give it effect. Effectively, this meant that in most instances the Shari'a constitutional clause would remain dormant until made effective by statutory law. Nevertheless, at the political level, Shari'a clauses played an important symbolic role. In addition, Shari'a clauses were often cited by courts in resolving possible ambiguities in statutory law by referring to the principles of Islamic jurisprudence.

Other than the Shari'a clauses found in the constitutions of many Muslim nations, a large number of countries incorporated Islamic law in their civil codes as one of the sources of legal construction. Typically, there is a clause written into the civil code instructing judges to interpret a statute by referring to the explicit meaning of the words of the statute. In cases of ambiguity, a judge is instructed to refer first to the established principles of Islamic law, and second to the prevailing customary practices in the country. In several Muslim countries, in cases of statutory ambiguity, judges are instructed to refer to custom first, and then to Shari'a law. Such civil code Shari'a clauses have their biggest impact upon the commercial practices of Muslim countries, depending, for the most part, on the clarity and specificity of the statute being interpreted by a court.

The Purported Islamization of Laws in Iraq

After the Gulf War of 1991, and especially after the rebellions in the South and North, Saddam announced that he would implement Islamic law in Iraq, but he did so primarily as a legitimacy and popularity ploy. Saddam had systematically obliterated all Islamic, Sunni and Shi'i opposition, and especially after quelling the rebellions that plagued the country at the conclusion of the first Gulf War, Saddam had achieved notoriety for executing more Muslim scholars and jurists than any other leader in the modern history of Islam. Suddenly, the staunchly secular Saddam discovered religion and made a point of getting himself filmed performing his prayers, or would interrupt media interviews, announcing that he must pause for prayers. Saddam's implementation of Islamic law was equally theatrical. On occasion, he would announce that a group of individuals will have their hands cut off for theft, or will be executed for adultery. The carrying out of these punishments were something of public spectacle, in which people would be forced to watch the gruesome affair at the risk of being shot. Since the charges and trials, and often even the names and identities of the suspects were not made public, strong suspicions persisted that those being punished were actually people accused of being opponents of the regime. It is not an exaggeration to conclude that since the late 1970's the Iraqi legal experience can be summed up as the following: There was no rule of law in Iraq, but only the rule of fear.

Comparative Models Regarding the Role of Islam in the Constitutions of Modern Muslim States and a Cost and Benefit Analysis of Each Model

Considering the wide range of technical and symbolic roles that Islam, in general, and Islamic law, in particular, have come to play in the world, it is useful to summarize the dynamics between Islam and the modern state in four basic models. These models will help place the various constitutional experiences, as far as Islam is concerned, in comparative perspective. In the process of explaining the four models, I will also analyze some of the costs and benefits associated with each. This will enable us to better assess the risks associated with any particular policy implemented in modern day Iraq.

Number One: The Strict-Separationist Model

According to this model, there is strict separation between Islam and the state. The state represents purely secular interests, and religion is not formally integrated in the political or legal system. Although the country in question might be predominately Muslim, there is no reference to Islam in the constitution or civil code, and personal laws are not based on nor inspired by Shari'a law. In this model, religious scholars and institutions may exist as a part of civil society, and they may even receive limited subsidies from the state, but they do not play an institutional role in the power structure, and they do not formally participate in formulating policy or the production of law.

This model, however, has not been widely adopted in Muslim countries. The prime examples of such a model are Turkey, Mauritania, Albania, and some of the former Soviet republics. Usually this model engenders wide opposition, and therefore, it tends to require heavy-handed repression by the state. Alternatively, as is the case with Turkey, it requires the dissemination of a widely popular civic ideology, such as Attaturkism, which thoroughly revises and reinvents the inherited cultural and religious convictions and practices. In the case of the former Soviet republics and Albania, this ideological role was played by Communism.

It is debatable whether this model is necessary for the existence of a liberal democracy. While all democracies generally recognize the necessity of separation between religion and state, according to this model, the separation is strict, dogmatic, and unwavering. Religion is not accommodated in any facet of public life, and the state has no religious identity whatsoever—it is not Muslim, Christian, or Jewish. The state does not fund religious institutions, and does not participate in any public displays of religion. But not all democracies have found it necessary to maintain a rigidly separationist policy as far as religion is concerned. Poland, Israel, India, and even England cannot be considered strict separationists, although they have managed to establish strong democratic systems. These four countries, and many others, have a very complex dynamic, where the government does not rule in God's name, but it does accommodate various aspects of religious practice and identity. In these countries, although the government guarantees the rights of all religious minorities, the government is not entirely impartial towards all religions. Even more, the countries, these governments represent, might even have a certain religious identity, such as Jewish, Catholic, or Protestant.

While the strict separationist model can guarantee absolute equality of religious freedom, its uncompromising secularism often puts it at odds with the religiously based sentiments of the majority of citizens. If the majority of the citizenry has a strong sense of religious identity, often the state is forced to clash with the sentiments of the majority, and as a result, the state ends up using heavy-handed tactics, largely at the expense of human rights. Consequently, the state becomes alienated from its citizenry, and the country exists in a perpetual condition of political turmoil and instability.

Number Two: The Accommodationist Model

This is the model adopted by a large number of Muslim countries including nations such as Syria, Algeria, Tunisia, and Iraq. In general, the institutions of the state are separated from religion, and Shari'a is excluded as a formal source of law. The personal and family law codes, however, are based on Islamic law, and are implemented by Shari'a courts. Although the constitution may assert the Muslim character of the nation, Shari'a is not indicated as a source or the source of legislation. In addition, the impact of Islamic legal precepts or precedents upon the commercial and civil codes is very limited. The most distinctive aspect of this model is that except for the personal and family law fields, Islamic law is not integrated in the mechanisms of the state, and Islam does not provide the guiding principles for the polity. Islam is accommodated in the sense that it dominates the field of inheritance, marriage, and divorce, and Islamic religious practices are permitted to exist, and often thrive, as a part of civil society, but the state does not actively promote the precepts of the religion, and does not give religious parties or interests a formal role in governance. In the Accommodationist Model, the religious endowments, usually inherited from previous eras, are allowed to exist, but they are placed under state control, and are permitted a very limited degree of autonomy. Mosques are often licensed and administered by the state, and imams (preachers who perform the call for prayer and lead prayer) are typically appointed by the state as well. Usually, the state will determine the appropriate subjects and content of the Friday sermons given in these mosques.

At the official and formal levels, this model keeps religion at a considerable arms length. But there are two distinctive risks in this model. Like the strict separationist model, it could generate considerable amount of religious opposition, and lead to a polarizing confrontation with Islamist forces. The other risk, and the more subtle one, is that unwittingly it could lead to considerable involvement with religion. Often in an effort to limit the popularistic and charismatic potential of the religion, the state is forced to involve itself with the regulation of religious expression, which, in turn, could invite greater repressive powers by the state.

Number Three: The Integrationist Model

In this model, there is greater formal involvement by the state with religion, but the political institutions continue to maintain their autonomy and separate existence from the religious institutions. Particularly in the decade of the 1970's, this model became more widespread and influential. Currently, examples of the integrationist model may be found in Egypt, the United Arab Emirates, Kuwait, Oman, Pakistan, Bangladesh, and Indonesia. The distinctive paradigm of this model is that while the state does not seek to implement all the technical prescriptions of Islamic law, and the state does not pretend to be the enforcer of canonical Islam, Islam and the Shari'ah are recognized as formal sources of moral and ethical inspiration. Furthermore, within the contextual limits of each country, there is an effort to integrate Islamic legal principles not just in the civil and commercial law fields, but also as they pertain to social justice, and public ethical norms. As mentioned above, Islamic law is identified as one of the main sources of legislation in the constitutional framework of the country, and the jurisprudential tradition of Islam could be referenced in order to resolve possible ambiguities in statutory law. Pursuant to this model, however, Islamic law is not self-executing, and Shari'a is considered a second frame of reference after statutory law. Therefore, only in the absence of statutory law on point will courts resort to Shari'a law or customary law, and in most countries judges are given guidance on which of the two, Shari'a or custom, is to take priority. Considering the vastness of the Islamic legal tradition, some countries instruct judges to apply a particular school of thought, for instance, the Hanafi School, or even to refer to a particular text, for instance, the Hidayah and/or the Majalla. In principle, it is possible for this instruction to vary from one province to another, within a single country, in order to accommodate the demographic differences within the country. For instance, in the absence of statutory law judges in one province may refer to Hanafi jurisprudence, while in a different province judges may refer to Ja'fari jurisprudence. Because Islamic law is applicable only in the absence of statutory law, and possibly in the absence of customary law as well, at the national level, the differences in legal application will be minor and technical.

There are many potential institutional frameworks that make it possible to formally integrate the ethical and moral principles of Islam without creating a theocratic state in which a group of religion experts override the will and choice of the people. For instance, a group of religious scholars may contribute input to proposed legislation, but without having veto power over such law making efforts. Such a group of religious scholars may be elected or appointed to the legislative or parliamentary body, and may constitute a percentage of such body. In this fashion, the religious scholars may comment directly on proposed legislation, and their view of what is Islamically acceptable or mandated may be given due consideration. In several countries, especially if appointed by the executive, this group of religious scholars does not have the power to vote on legislation, but are given an opportunity to comment or advocate a particular point of view. In some countries, instead of reserving a place for religious scholars in the legislative branch, there is a separate body, often at the level of ministry, which is regularly consulted by the legislative body and asked to comment on proposed legislation. The comments of this religious consultative body are either read or distributed in the legislature or parliament, and are often printed and published as well.

The earmark of the integrationist model is that, on principle, it does not seek to exclude Islam from the public manifestations of life. However, the Integrationist Model formally recognizes Islam's leading ethical and social educational role, and it allows Islam to manifest itself in public life through the personal convictions and commitments of lawmakers. Importantly, the Integrationist Model's consistent with the historical experience of Islam, and the traditional role of Shari'a. The Qur'an itself asserts that there can be no coercion or duress in religion, and the Integrationist Model attempts to avoid transforming religion into the coercive instrument of the state. It also attempts to avoid institutionalizing a particular group of spokesmen as the enforcers of the Divine Will. In addition, the Integrationist Model tends to respect the enormous diversity and richness of the Islamic jurisprudential tradition by refusing to enforce one particular view to the exclusion of all others.

The main shortcoming of the Integrationist Model is that at the level of political symbolism, this model is not always capable of leveraging itself politically in order to emphasize its consistency with Islamic paradigms. In other words, because the state does not position itself as the strict enforcer of the Divine law, at times, it is challenging for the state to avail itself of the perception of Islamic authenticity and legitimacy. However, this model is not as vulnerable to accusations of being disconnected from its Islamic heritage, or accusations of excluding Islam from public life, as the previous two models.

Number Four: The Requisitionist Model

This model is the closest to a theocratic government, except for the fact that there is no consecrated church in Islam. The state selects the canonical doctrine, which the state believes represents the correct Islamic position, and enforces it both as the will of the state and God. This model has been adopted by a few countries, which include Saudi Arabia, Iran, and for a period of time, Sudan. The Requisitionist Model has taken different shapes and forms, some of which are able to achieve a greater degree of democratic practices than others. For instance, Iran gives a council of jurist-consuls and other high-ranking clergymen a near absolute veto power over legislation and policy. In Saudi Arabia, the executive empowers the judiciary to implement Islamic law, assisted by executive orders or regulations that dictate policy or particular limits. The important element in this model is that depending upon one's perspective, the state is requisitioned in the service of religion, or religion is requisitioned in the service of state. In all cases, there is an institutional body that determines the Will of God, and enforces it as such. As such, typically in this model, all courts are considered Shari'a courts charged with the enforcement of Islamic law, as defined by the state. Courts follow the instructions of the state as to what constitutes Islamic law, and in some cases and in particular fields, courts are granted wide law making powers.

The difficulty with this model is two-fold: One, an institution or group of institutions becomes empowered with the gloss of divinity, and therefore, it is very difficult to reconcile this model with democracy. Second, this model tends to narrowly define orthodoxy because it favors one particular Islamic perspective over all others. Arguably, this has the serious potential of undermining the richness and diversity of the Islamic tradition.

The Spectrum of Models

It is important to note that the four models identified here are approximations of the earmarks of actual practices of modern Muslim states. However, there is a spectrum that exists within each model and between one model and the other. Therefore, it is possible that an Accommodationist state borders on being Integrationist, and it is also possible that an Integrationist state would act as Requisitionist over some issues and under certain circumstances. For example, Egypt, over most issues, is Integrationist, but at times, acting upon the instructions of the Azhar University, it bans certain books that it considers religiously offensive. In those instants, it is acting pursuant to the Requisitionist model. Furthermore, some countries, such as Jordan, have experimented with the Integrationist model but of lately have drifted towards the Accommodationist model. On the other hand, for example, Sudan has drifted from a Requisitionist orientation to a more integrationist stance.

The Case of Iraq and the Iraqi Constitution

There is little doubt that many Iraqis are aspiring for a democratic order that would guard against the kind of abuses that they for long have had to endure. The formidable challenges confronting Iraqis include how to overcome the absolute jurisprudential impoverishment that they suffered under the Ba'ath, while reclaiming their creative legacy; how to find justice in post-Saddam Iraq, while avoiding the destructiveness of vengeance; and how to make the law a shield and tool in the hands of the people; and not an oppressive sword in the hands of the state. On the legal front, the challenge will be how to establish order and stability, while still allowing the law to be an agent of progressive change. It is important in this regard to note that the rule of law is a necessary condition for a democracy to exist, but it is not enough. Democracy is not just about the objectivity and fairness of process or the division and separation of power between various branches of the government. Democracy is also not just about giving effect to will of the majority, or accountability to the people. Democracy is about a moral commitment to the fundamental and basic worth and dignity of each and every member of the citizenry, and the conscientious engineering of government and society so as to make human beings secure in their rights.

Importantly, this moral commitment can be expressed through law, but it cannot be not created or invented by legal command. Democracy is not secured by drafting good laws alone, but it must be made a part of one's cultural and ethical view. Considering Iraq's rich civilizational heritage, there is no doubt that Iraqis will be looking, and rightly so, into their pre-Ba'th legal and moral history for inspiration and guidance on how to make the moral commitment and develop the ethical worldview necessary for a democracy. In this context, it is important for American policy makers to understand that Iraq's legal and ethical history did not start with the overthrow of Saddam. A major component of the Iraqi heritage is the Islamic faith, and the leading role that Iraq played in the development of Islamic law. But here is where Iraq's creative legacy is most needed. A dual commitment to Islamic law and democracy is possible, but only if Muslims understand Islamic law to reinforce the same commitments made by democracy to individual human rights and dignities. This is exactly where Iraq might be able to reclaim its leading educative and inspirational role towards the rest of the Muslim world. It will be a revolutionary step if Iraqi legal minds are able to reinterpret and rethink the Islamic classical tradition in a way that upholds the basic individual rights necessary for a democratic order.

Opting for either the Strict-Separationist or Requisitionist (theocratic) Models in Iraq will be nothing short of a disaster for the Iraqi people, Muslims, in general, and the West. The establishment of a theocracy in Iraq will inevitably lead to a denial of human rights, the marginalization and exclusion of Iraq from the world community, and considerable sectarian tensions between Shi'i and Sunni Muslims. But even more, a theocracy is an affront to the wisdom of Islam, the diversity and richness of Shari'a, and to the historical legacy and established precedent of Muslims around the world. But the forcible exclusion of Islam from public life, state sponsorship, and all legal and constitutional documents will be a disaster of equal proportions. The worse thing that the government of the United States can possibly do, while acting as an occupying power in Iraq, is to impose upon the Iraqi people a political condition that is so artificial—that is so alien to the collective consciousness of the Iraqis, and that is at odds with their historical experience and aspirations—that it appears that the United States is, in fact, acting like a power of occupation and domination, not persuasion and liberation. The danger is that if the United States appears hostile or insensitive to the religious sentiments of the Iraqis, this will invite resistance. It will be a real tragedy if the democratic experiment in Iraq fails, not because the Iraqis do not believe in democracy, but because democracy is seen as part of the ideological package of an aggressive or imperialistic occupying force.

The United States government must successfully communicate to the Iraqi people its desire to help them to practice their religion, if they so desire, more fully and freely, not force upon them a situation that they will view as hostile, deprecating, or insensitive towards their faith based commitments and beliefs. More concretely, the United States government should not resist, and, in fact, should tolerate and support, any efforts by the Iraqis to (1) define the religious identity of their country; (2) preserve the sanctity and inviolability of Islamic law in certain areas of legal practice that the Iraqis define as highly personal and intimate to their identity and will as a people; and (3) define Islam in such a way that it is consistent with democracy and human rights. For instance, if the Iraqis wish to proclaim a bill of individual rights, in their constitutional document, and further wish to assert that this bill of rights is derived from their Islamic commitments and understandings, the United States should encourage such a move. The United States government ought not be suspicious of any effort by the Iraqis to anchor their human rights and democratic commitments in novel or original interpretations of the Islamic tradition. It should be noted that I am not advocating that the government of the United States dictate any Islamic positions or establish any religious doctrine. The key here is that whatever efforts are made on behalf of Islam must be driven by Iraqis themselves. I am only addressing possible responses or reactions by our government to anticipated Iraqi initiatives on behalf of their religious identity and faith. If the Iraqis are able to articulate their democratic and human rights choices in terms of Islamically compelling positions, this will have the long-term advantage of transforming the Iraqi experience into a normative precedent for all Muslim nations. If Iraqis can successfully establish that it is their Islamic faith that inspired them to commit to democracy and human rights, this is bound to have a far reaching impact upon Muslim countries and nations around the globe, and United States would have played the role of partnership and sponsorship in generating this pivotal development in Muslim history.

The Japanese and German Post World War II Model and the Democratic Challenge in Iraq

When evaluating the chances of democracy in Iraq, in many ways, the establishment of capitalist democracies in Germany and Japan in the Post World War II period becomes an encouraging precedent. One can rightly take pride in the transformation of these two countries into democratic world powers under American sponsorship. The precedent of both these countries does indicate that democracy can be taught and transplanted, and that it does not necessarily have to emerge through the natural socio-political processes within a particular country. There are, however, several elements that counsel against assuming that whatever worked in Germany and Japan will necessarily work in Iraq. The following are some of these elements of difference and distinction:

1. Both countries before their democratic transformation were heavily industrialized countries with advanced economies and very high productivity. The United States was able to inject capital into the war torn, but developed, economies of both countries, and by doing so, the United States was able to re-set both nations on their path of economic progress. Although highly despotic governments dominated both Germany and Japan, there were strong, developed, and sophisticated entrepreneurial classes ready and set to share

power once these despotic governments fell. In this regard, the situation in Iraq is markedly different. Iraq is not an industrialized or technologically advanced country. Furthermore, Saddam had severely weakened the entrepreneurial class and forced them into a symbiotic relationship with the state in which they were more like economic leeches heavily dependent on a very corrupt government for their survival. This is bound to make the distribution of economic base and power in Iraq more challenging, and will require a much heavier investment of venture capital in order to create a productive economic system that can support a democracy.

2. Levels of literacy, education, and technological development were already very high at the time of the American occupation of Japan and West Germany. Democracy is much better secure and supported in societies enjoying a high level of literacy and education. Literacy and education contribute to the creation of sophisticated civil societies and are conducive to the development of civic virtues, such as social and political responsibility, accountability, compromise, and the sharing of power, which are importing for nourishing and guarding a democracy. Literacy and education levels in Iraq, although higher than some of the countries in the region, are low when compared to West German and Japanese standards.
3. Historically, both Germany and Japan were colonizing, not colonized, nations. Unlike Iraq, Germany and Japan did not have to deal with a collective historical memory that labors under the trauma of colonialism. This meant that both countries were relatively more receptive to the influx of ideas and influences coming from the United States, specifically, and the West, more generally. Unlike Iraq, there was no national trauma induced by long periods of occupation and domination, and a deeply ingrained sense of distrust and suspicion focused on the West.
4. Before the war, Germany and Japan followed a particular ideology that had become utterly undermined and discredited after World War II. The ideological defeat was complete and thorough, and the German's and Japanese were ready for an ideological transformation. In the case of Iraq, even if one asserts that the defeat of Ba'athism, the secular nationalist ideology of Saddam and the ruling government of Syria, is complete, Ba'athism is not the issue. The issue is the inclusion or exclusion of Islam in the constitutional document of Iraq. Not only is Islam not a discredited ideology, it is not an ideology at all. As a religious faith, it has its own set of demands on its followers. If the United States forces Iraqis into a position in which they have to choose between the demands of their religion and demands of their constitution, the constitutional document will not penetrate deeply into the socio-political fabric of Iraq, and these competing demands are bound to generate tensions and strong resistance.
5. Iraqis, as Arabs and Muslims, are firmly situated within a particular sociohistorical context. Iraq does not only influence the countries and people situated within its region, but is also, in turn, influenced by them. It is important that the United States not contribute to a situation in which Iraq becomes, by our decree, artificially alienated from its context. If Iraq's distinctive Muslim and Arab character is artificially diluted, and its policies become a replica of American preferences and policies, this will only confirm the status of Iraq as a country occupied by an alien power. Put differently, it is important to avoid giving the impression that Iraq is a mirror of the United States, and no longer authentically Iraqi. Such an impression is bound to further radicalize and polarize the region, and will in the long term, inevitably, backfire. The regional contexts of Germany and Japan were completely different. Any possible German or Japanese opposition to American policies could not gain inspiration or support from its regional surroundings. Obviously, the situation in Iraq is decisively different. It is important that in the process of saving Iraq, the United States does not end up losing the region.

Respecting the Iraqi Choice

These material differences, among many others, between Japan and Germany, on the one hand, and Iraq, on the other, are mentioned here to emphasize the distinctiveness and particularity of the challenge in Iraq. In my view, we cannot afford to deal with Iraq as the vanquishing victors, and expect the Iraqis to mold themselves after our image. It is important that the United States displays a considerable amount of sensitivity and respect for the Iraqi history, civilization, and religion. Therefore, it would be a serious mistake to deny Iraqis the opportunity to define themselves—even if this self-definition would include choices regarding the public role of religion that would not be our own.

Senator CORNYN. Thank you very much, Doctor.
Mr. Al-Sarraf.

STATEMENT OF SERMID AL-SARRAF, MEMBER, BOARD OF DIRECTORS, IRAQI JURISTS' ASSOCIATION

Mr. AL-SARRAF. Thank you, Chairman Cornyn, Chairman Chafee, Senator Feingold. I am pleased to be here today as a member of the Iraqi Jurists' Association, the Working Group on Transitional Justice with the State Department's Future of Iraq project, and as a Muslim-American attorney from California, to discuss the challenges which face Iraq and the Coalition Provisional Authority, the CPA, with regard to reestablishing the rule of law in this post-Saddam era.

Senator CORNYN. Could I ask you to pull the microphone a little closer to you so we can hear you a little better? I appreciate it.

Mr. AL-SARRAF. I'm not going to repeat the description of the IJA and its history. It's recorded in my written statement, which I will include with the record.

The challenges on the road to restoring the rule of law in Iraq can be broken down into two categories, those facing the Iraqi people, and those facing the Coalition Provisional Authority, or the CPA, and in particular, the role of the United States. The working group report, which was submitted to the committee and is fairly extensive in English and much more extensive in Arabic, roughly 750 pages, goes into great detail as to the challenges facing the Iraqi people, so I'll focus my time here today on those challenges that face the Coalition Provisional Authority and, in particular, the United States.

The three major challenges, as I see them, are: (1) delivering on promises, (2) applying appropriate resources to the task, and (3) understanding Iraqi society and enfranchising and empowering Iraqis themselves.

On delivering on promises, the U.S. has a small window of opportunity to make good on its promises before the situation in Iraq spirals out of control. A definitive success in Iraq may be the key to restoring our image as a Nation that stands for liberty, democracy, and respect for human rights both at home and abroad.

In the eyes of Iraqis inside Iraq, prior U.S. foreign policies were marked by broken promises, the most prominent of which was the one made immediately after the first Gulf War, which promised U.S. support for the Iraqi people if they were to rise up against Saddam. When they did, in overwhelming numbers, 14 of 18 provinces were liberated from Ba'ath party rule. The U.S. and other allied forces stood by and watched as Saddam Hussein brutally massacred tens of thousands of civilians to maintain his grip on power.

Now, while Iraqis are, on the whole, relieved and genuinely appreciative that Saddam was removed, they are also simultaneously wary of the coalition forces' true intentions. They ask the question, after supporting Saddam during the Iran-Iraq war, defeating him in Kuwait while tacitly supporting his efforts to stay in power and forcing devastating sanctions which ultimately strengthened his rule and punished the Iraqi people, what has changed?

It is critical that the CPA understand this backdrop and the environment in which it operates. The initial objective of moving in quickly with civilian and humanitarian assistance to effect an immediate improvement in the day-to-day living conditions was unquestionably the correct policy. Unfortunately, and without regard to root causes, in the areas of security, lack of electricity, telephones, and other basic services, this policy has not been fully achieved.

Because of this backdrop, there is very little room for delays and mistakes, which the Iraqi people perceive in the context of a continuum of past policies. In terms of applying the appropriate resources to the task, I'd like to describe this challenge by way of a specific example taken from the front page of the *Washington Post* on May 21, 2003, in an article entitled, "Ad-Libbing Iraq's Infrastructure."

One of the examples of this ad-libbing was the case of the courts in the southern city of Najaf. A recent law school student, an Army reservist from Wisconsin, without deference to the State of Wisconsin, with 1 year of training in Arabic, was tasked with reestablishing the courts in the city. One of the first actions that was taken was to have all of the lawyers vote on the judges, whether they would keep their positions. For perspective, if this was done in L.A. Superior Court, I can guarantee you that many of the lawyers would not be voting for the most qualified or most impartial judges.

This is not a knock on the service person. In fact, she made significant advances in involving women jurists, to her credit. She is simply executing her orders to the best of her ability. This is a critique of the policy, however, that fails to understand and appreciate the needs and apply the appropriate resources to the task.

This is not an isolated incident. In early May, the Department of Justice sent a judicial assessment team to Iraq. Not one of the roughly 11 members of this team were Iraqi legal professionals, or even native Iraqi Arabic speakers, despite the fact that the DOJ conducted a 2-week training program on international humanitarian law just a few weeks prior to 25 to 30 prominent Iraqi jurists.

Today, you saw in the *Washington Post*, I'm sure, the article about the military versus the civilian reconstruction and the problems that the military was having in rising to the occasion, and this is not a plug for the *Washington Post*, by the way, but if I were a jurist inside Iraq witnessing these events, I would think to myself that the CPA and the U.S. are not taking this task seriously, and this is not for lack of expertise.

The U.S. has access to, particularly in the State Department and the Future of Iraq project, many, many experts, and unfortunately the rifts between the various departments within the U.S. Government have stymied these efforts.

The third challenge, understanding Iraqi society and enfranchising Iraqis, part of the problem with assessing the appropriate resources is a fundamental lack of understanding of Iraqi society, its history, and its people. Many assumptions are made based on experiences of other countries, such as Afghanistan, post-World War II Germany, and Japan.

Iraqi is a country with a legal tradition which predates Saddam Hussein and the Ba'ath Party. Its legal system is based on a combination of Shari'ah law derived from the Ottoman era and civil law derived from the French legal code. Among its people are highly qualified legal professionals, judges, lawyers, prosecutors and law professors both inside and outside the country.

Piecing together a legal framework for this transition period is not as complex as the example of Afghanistan and, unlike Germany and Japan of the World War II era, Iraqis did not elect nor freely accept the Ba'ath Party nor Saddam's regime. The main victims of Saddam's regime were his own people, and they sacrificed greatly in numerous attempts to rid themselves of this regime. The vast majority of lower level members of the Ba'ath Party joined not out of loyalty or belief, but out of dire necessity or fear of death.

How did this understanding change the CPA's approach? First, most Iraqis are more than happy and willing to participate and take the lead in the de-Ba'athification process. The Iraqi people do not need to be convinced about the evils of the prior regime. They know it, they lived it, and many died because of it. It is critical not to disenfranchise those who would otherwise be supporters. This has happened with the disbanding of the military, with hundreds of thousands of people dependent upon their salaries for their basic survival.

Second, among Iraqis themselves are qualified professionals, with sound reputations both inside and outside Iraq. It is critical that the CPA tap into this important resource. I know that this effort has begun in certain ministries, but it needs to continue and expand. Iraqis in particular in the legal field are very sensitive about outside involvement in the Arab world, especially if they are from countries perceived to have benefited or cooperated with the prior regime. Even for exiled Iraqis, their role should be limited to advising, consulting, and assisting, and not include positions of authority unless specifically elected by the people themselves in free and open elections.

Based on my conversations with trusted exiles, trusted sources in-country, Iraqis are feeling like strangers in their own country. Either through neglect, lack of understanding, or for the sake of expediency, current efforts seem to be avoiding direct Iraqi involvement and their opinions in important decisions.

Disbanding the military in such a manner is one such example, and I'd like to just respond to one of the comments about reducing the number of Ba'ath Party members in the exclusion from or lustration from government service. While I agree that their families need to be supported, and the measures should be looked at to extend their benefits and their salaries, I think there should be no wavering on the principle of excluding Ba'ath Party members from public office.

Senator CORNYN. We want to make sure we get a chance to ask questions and so forth. Could I ask you, please, to wrap up your original comments?

Mr. AL-SARRAF. Yes.

Senator CORNYN. And then we will, of course, be able to allow you to expand on that as we ask questions.

Mr. AL-SARRAF. I'll wrap up with the quote that I made from your prior speech.

Senator CORNYN. Please.

Mr. AL-SARRAF. These are not insurmountable challenges. I am optimistic for one simple reason, and that is, to echo your words, after defeating our enemies in World War II, we left behind constitutions and representative government, not permanent military authority, and we can do the same in Iraq.

Because of this tradition, the U.S. is uniquely positioned to succeed in this important undertaking. Any failures in Iraq reflect on all of us and will have a long-lasting negative impact on U.S. interests in Iraq, the region, and the rest of the world. Iraqis do not make distinctions between the Pentagon and the State Department, Democrats or Republicans. This is a massive undertaking which requires the best talents of all.

Thank you.

[The prepared statement of Mr. Al-Sarraf follows:]

PREPARED STATEMENT OF SERMID AL-SARRAF, ESQ.

Chairman Cornyn, Chairman Chafee, Senator Feingold, Senator Boxer and, Members of the joint Subcommittees, I am pleased to be here today as a member of the Iraqi Jurists' Association, the Working Group on Transitional Justice of the State Department's Future of Iraq project, and a Muslim American attorney from California, to discuss the challenges which face Iraq and the Coalition Provisional Authority (CPA) with regard to re-establishing the Rule of Law in this post-Saddam era.

The Iraqi Jurists' Association (IJA) was formed almost 3 years ago and was the largest consortium of Iraqi judges, lawyers, prosecutors and law professors outside Iraq. Last year, IJA teamed up with the State Department's Future of Iraq project to form the Working Group on Transitional Justice which, in turn, prepared a 750 page report entitled "The Road to Re-establishing Rule of Law and Restoring Civil Society—A Blueprint." This report, originally in the Arabic language, was finalized and adopted on March 23, 2003. A summary of this report in English was also prepared. The Working Group and the report itself benefited from internationally recognized experts in the area of Transitional Justice such as Professor Cherif Bassiouni, President of the International Human Rights Law Institute at DePaul University; Professor Alex Boraine, President of the International Transitional Justice Center, former deputy chair of the Truth and Reconciliation Commission in South Africa; Mr. Neil Kritz, Director of the Rule of Law Program at the U.S. Institute of Peace; and many others.

Now, with more than 80 prominent legal personalities and after a recent trip to Iraq by the IJA chairman, Dr. Tariq Ali Al-Saleh, the organization is in the process of transferring its headquarters from London to Baghdad where it is expected that Iraqi jurists from inside the country will take the lead in transforming the IJA into an effective civic institution with a mission to help create, educate and defend an independent judiciary.

The challenges on the road to restoring the Rule of Law in Iraq can be broken down into two categories: (1) those facing the Iraqi people and (2) those facing the Coalition Provisional Authority (CPA), in particular the role of the United States. The Working Group report goes into great detail as to the challenges facing the Iraqi people. I will spend my time here today, addressing what I believe are the challenges to the CPA and the U.S. in particular.

The three major challenges I see are:

1. Delivering on Promises
2. Applying Appropriate Resources to the Task
3. Understanding Iraqi Society and Enfranchising Iraqis

1. Delivering on Promises

The U.S. has a small window of opportunity to make good on its promises before the situation in Iraq spirals out of control. A definitive success in Iraq may be the key to restoring our image as a nation that stands for liberty, democracy and respect for human rights, both at home and abroad.

In the eyes of Iraqis inside Iraq, prior U.S. foreign policy was marked by broken promises, the most prominent of which was the one made immediately after the first Gulf war, which promised U.S. support for the Iraqi people if they were to rise up against Saddam. When they did in overwhelming numbers (14 of 18 provinces were liberated from Ba'ath party rule), the U.S. and other allied forces watched by as Saddam brutally massacred tens of thousands of civilians to maintain his grip on power.

Now, while Iraqis are on the whole relieved and genuinely appreciative that Saddam was removed, they are also simultaneously wary about the coalition forces' "true" intentions behind this action. They ask the question, after supporting Saddam during the Iran-Iraq war, defeating him in Kuwait but tacitly supporting his efforts to stay in power, enforcing devastating sanctions which ultimately strengthened his rule and punished the Iraqi people, what has changed?

It is critical that the CPA understand this backdrop and the environment in which it operates. The initial objective of moving in quickly with civilian and humanitarian assistance to effect an immediate improvement in the day to day living conditions was unquestionably the correct policy. Unfortunately, and without regard to root causes, in the areas of security, lack of electricity, telephones and other basic services this policy has not been fully achieved. Because of this backdrop, there is very little room for delays and mistakes, which the Iraqi people perceive in the context of a continuum of past policies.

2. Applying Appropriate Resources to the Task

I'd like to describe this challenge by way of a specific example taken from the front page of the *Washington Post* on May 21, 2003, in an article entitled, *Ad-Libbing Iraq's Infrastructure.* One of the examples of this "Ad-Libbing" was the case of the courts in the southern city of Najaf. A recent law school student and Army reservist from Wisconsin with 1 year of training in Arabic was tasked with re-establishing the courts in this city. One of the first actions was to have all of the lawyers vote on which judges would keep their positions. For perspective, if this were done in Los Angeles Superior Court, I can guarantee you that many lawyers would not be voting for the best qualified, most impartial judges. This is not a knock on this service person, she is executing her orders to the best of her ability. This is a critique of the policy that fails to understand and appreciate the needs and apply the appropriate resources to the task.

This is not an isolated incident. In early May, the Department of Justice sent a judicial assessment team to Iraq. Not one of the roughly 11 members of the team were Iraqi legal professionals (or even native Iraqi-Arabic speakers), despite the fact that the DOJ conducted a 2-week training program on international humanitarian law for 25–30 prominent Iraqi jurists in late March.

If I were a jurist inside Iraq, witnessing these events, I would think to myself that the CPA and/or the U.S. are not taking this task seriously.

3. Understanding Iraqi Society and Enfranchising Iraqis

Part of the problem with assessing the appropriate resources is a fundamental lack of understanding of Iraqi society, its history and its people. Many assumptions are made based on experiences in other countries, such as Afghanistan, post World War II Germany, and Japan, etc.

Iraq is a country with a legal tradition which predates Saddam Hussein and the Ba'ath party. Its legal system is based on a combination of Shari'ah law (derived from the Ottoman era) and Civil law (derived from the French legal code). Among its people are highly qualified legal professionals: judges, lawyers, prosecutors and law professors, both inside and outside the country. Piecing together a legal framework for this transitional period is not as complex as in the example of Afghanistan.

And, unlike Germany and Japan of the WWII era, Iraqis did not elect nor freely accept the Ba'ath party nor Saddam's regime. The main victims of Saddam's regime were his own people and they sacrificed greatly in numerous attempts to rid themselves of this regime. The vast majority of lower level members of the Ba'ath party joined not out of belief or loyalty but out of dire necessity or fear of death.

How does this understanding change the CPA's approach? First, most Iraqis are more than happy and willing to participate in and take the lead in the de-ba'athification process. The Iraqi people do not need to be convinced about the evils of the prior regime: they know it, they lived it, and many died because of it. It is critical not to disenfranchise those who would otherwise be supporters. This has happened with the disbanding of the military, with hundreds of thousands of people dependent upon their salaries for their basic survival.

Second, among Iraqis themselves there are qualified professionals with sound reputations both inside and outside Iraq. It is critical that the CPA tap into this important resource. I know that this effort has begun in certain Ministries, but it needs to continue and expand. Iraqis, in particular in the legal field, are very sensitive about outside involvement, including from the Arab world especially if they are from countries perceived to have benefited or cooperated with the prior regime. Even for exiled Iraqis, their role should be limited to advising, consulting and assisting and not include positions of authority unless specifically elected by the people themselves in free and open elections.

Based on my conversations with trusted sources in-country, Iraqis are feeling like strangers in their own country. Either through neglect, lack of understanding, or for the sake of expediency, current efforts seem to be avoiding direct Iraqi involvement and their opinions in important decisions. Disbanding the military in such a manner is one such example.

This must not happen with the formation of the constitution. To ensure maximum participation in this process, some jurists in the IJA recommend a multi-phased process. The first phase would be to hold a national referendum on the form of government (as an example, whether it would be a republic, parliamentary or presidential system, constitutional monarchy, etc.) and once that decision is made by the Iraqi people, a group of elected representatives could be formed to draft the constitution with the assistance of international and domestic legal experts. To protect the long term stability of a democratic Iraq, there would need to be a strong and independent judiciary with a mandate to review the constitutionality of actions of the other two branches of government.

Conclusion

These are not insurmountable challenges. I am optimistic for one simple reason and that is, if I may echo the words of Chairman Cornyn in one of his recent speeches:

> After defeating our enemies in World War II, we left behind constitutions and representative government, not permanent military authorities—and we can do the same in Iraq.—*from a speech to the American Enterprise Institute, 6/10/2003*

Because of this tradition, the U.S. is uniquely positioned to succeed in this important undertaking. Any failures in Iraq reflect on all of us and will have a long-lasting, negative impact on U.S. interests in Iraq, the region and the rest of the world. Iraqis do not make distinctions between the Pentagon or the State Department, Democrats or Republicans. This is a massive undertaking which requires the best talents of all. The consequences of success and/or failure will also be shared by all.

Senator CORNYN. Thank you very much.
Ms. Salbi.

STATEMENT OF ZAINAB SALBI, PRESIDENT AND FOUNDER, WOMEN FOR WOMEN INTERNATIONAL

Ms. SALBI. Yes, thank you very much for this opportunity. It is indeed an honor and a privilege to be here. I am speaking here not only in my capacity as president of Women for Women International, or as an Iraqi-American, but as someone who recently came back from Iraq. I had been there both in January to get an assessment of pre-war Iraq and what Iraqis are saying, and then I recently came from Iraq in May, where I got an assessment and interviews of different socioeconomic classes, ethnic and religious backgrounds all over Iraq, mostly in central and southern Iraq.

So what I'm trying to say is, I'm trying to convey what the Iraqis are saying, including those who I talked to up until 2 days ago from Baghdad.

I called my original report, *Please Tell Mr. Bush,* because a lot of people were following and telling me, "please tell Mr. Bush thank you for liberating us from Saddam, for getting rid of Saddam once and for all," so there is a great level of appreciation that Iraqis have finally been liberated from 35 years of oppression.

Having said that, they will always continue the sentence and say, "and we need more." Iraqis had and still have high expectations from America, and some of these expectations may be too much. There are expectations that there is a Marshall Plan going to be in Iraq, and the impact of the plan will be seen in a couple of months' period, and that is obviously, some of them are not realistic. What we need here is to address these expectations and do something about them.

Economically, although I do have to acknowledge Ambassador Bremer's accomplishments in terms of reinstating the salaries, including to former military personnel, that has a huge economic impact on the Iraqis. However, small- and middle- and medium-sized businesses have not been operating for 4 months now, and they do have a huge impact on those who are dependent on daily wages. The economy is switching from local production to export dependence, and that is impacting the long-term economic sustainability of Iraq.

A lot of people are complaining that the American and coalition forces started by talking about democracy rather than talking about economic reconstruction. I'll summarize what one man told me in a small alley in Najaf, a very conservative province in southern Iraq, who said, we need food and security before democracy. When you save someone from death, his first wish is not a car, but basic needs to regain his energy. Americans, God bless them, are more concerned with democracy than they are with addressing our basic needs.

He continues and says, we need economic stability as a prerequisite for democracy. We need to be able to breathe so we can talk about how we can build our democratic process. He wasn't denying the importance of democracy, as much as saying, I need a break now.

There is a huge impact on women in post-war Iraq. The security situation, which continues to be very chaotic, to say the least, is having particular impact on women, who are being targeted for kidnapping. Rumors in Iraq, and confirmed by actually an article in *The Economist,* there's a market now where women are being sold and trafficked in Baghdad itself. This is impeding the women's movement outside the house, and this is critical, especially when we have such a high percentage of single heads of households after 20 years of wars.

Political participation for women is very limited. While a lot of the local political parties, as well as those from exile, have very few, if any, women's representation in their parties, when they address this issue they don't seem to have an ideological opposition to it as much as, this didn't occur to them.

A lot of Iraqi women, though, are very adamant about their participation in the political and reconstruction process. A 40-year-old woman, as one of the middle-class women who wears the traditional head scarves, was telling me, I want Iraqi women to be part of every process of building the country, in the army, in sport, in every single sector. Women need to have 50 percent representation in the country. I wish this could happen. We deserve that, and we have the credibility to do that as well as men.

We have to incorporate women's participation in the constitutional discussion and the political discussion as well as in the economic reconstruction in Iraq, without which we will not have sustainable economic development or political development in Iraq.

As to political parties, there is a sense—well, I'll summarize what one man told me. He said, "before we had one Saddam, and now we have many, many Saddams who use power in similar ways of Saddam Hussein." A lot of the political parties who came from exile are known to have, or are perceived to have a monopoly of discussions and dialog with the CPA and with coalition forces.

There is no sense of transparency. There is no sense of people knowing even what is happening, and the lack of information, I would say, is at the core of the problem. People need to know what is happening, and there is no medium of communication with the average person in Iraq, and this is again a lot of the complaints. I summarize again what one person told me. He said, we need to know what is going on, we need a public relations campaign that can speak to the concerns of the average Iraqi.

Another person said the same thing. We need to know what is going on. We don't want to see soldiers killing two people every day, or American soldiers being killed for that matter. America needs to focus its communication to the average Iraqi, the real Iraqi, by helping them resume their daily work and daily lives to a normal stage. Real people need to get a sense that America is communicating with them and addressing their concerns. If you lose the average person, you will lose peace in Iraq.

This is what an Iraqi just told me, actually a businessman, 2 days ago. He said we are at the risk at this point of not only losing the average person in Iraq, we are at the risk of losing the elite of Iraq. When everyone's business is being impacted, when the economy is being impacted, and when there is no sense of communication and transparency of what is happening, we are at the risk of losing these people, the Iraqis, and when we lose the Iraqis, we will lose peace in Iraq.

There is a strong sense by the Iraqis themselves, communicate, communicate, communicate to us. There are only 2 hours of TV over there. This is not enough. They need to hear from the coalition forces what is going on. A PR campaign would be a critical one.

We also need to make sure that we have a transparent process. We need to include the expertise of Iraqis internally. I completely agree with my colleagues in here. Those of us who are in exile can only be advisors. Those Iraqis who are in Iraqi are the only legitimate people to run the country. They have suffered, and they need to have a say in what's going on.

Senator CORNYN. Ms. Salbi, let me ask you please, if you would, wind up your opening statement so we can get some questions. I regret to say that we do have a very large Medicare bill making its way through the Senate, so we will have to stop for some votes and come back in a little bit, but please, if you will conclude, and then we will go to questions until it's necessary for us to go.

Ms. SALBI. The last thing is, we need to do an awe and shock campaign in economic development in Iraq. This is the only way we can win peace and security not only in Iraq, but throughout the whole Middle East, and women have to be at the core of that.

[The prepared statement of Ms. Salbi follows:]

PREPARED STATEMENT OF ZAINAB SALBI

Thank you for the opportunity to testify before the Congress at such a critical moment with respect to the current situation in Iraq and our attempts to build a lasting peace in the country. My remarks reflect more than 10 years of work in post conflict societies including Bosnia and Herzegovina, Kosova, Afghanistan and elsewhere, with a particular focus on women. In the case of Iraq, my remarks are informed by my own national origin, as I was born and raised in Iraq, and by two fact finding trips I have recently taken to Iraq on behalf of Women for Women International—one trip took place in January of this year to get a sense of the conditions and attitudes in pre-war Iraq. A more recent trip took place in May of this year as I prepared an assessment report on the current situation in Iraq as we work to open an office to help the women of Iraq through Women for Women International. In both trips, I interviewed women and men from different socio-economic backgrounds, ethnic groups and religious tendencies in both central and southern Iraq. Since then, I have maintained almost daily contacts with Iraqis, primarily in Baghdad. My ultimate goal for the report that follows is to convey an accurate image of what is going on in the hearts and minds of Iraqis, and particularly women. Only by having a clear understanding of what the actual conditions on the ground are can we work on our common goal of building a lasting peace, economic prosperity and a sustainable democracy in Iraq.

I will conclude by making recommendations that address the concerns of the Iraqis with whom I have met and who must be the new constituency as we move forward—the new constituency for American and international non-governmental organizations, international organizations such as the United Nations, and the Coalition Provisional Authority.

Regardless of how Iraqis felt about the war, one can safely argue that the vast majority of Iraqis welcomed the opportunity to get rid of Saddam Hussein's regime and are thankful for the Coalition's role and America's leadership in freeing Iraq. However, while Iraqis may have different visions for the future of Iraq, everyone with whom I spoke, without exception, is surprised at what is perceived to be the lack of any organization or preparation for post-war Iraq. This was most evidenced by the chaos and anarchy that spread across Iraq in the days and weeks after the war, and in the continuing inability of Coalition forces to fully restore basic services or provide physical security for the overwhelming majority of Iraqis.

The looting and burning of ministries, universities and other public properties, the limited electricity, lack of phone systems, extensive delay in resuming food delivery, the mass possession of guns and machine guns—among even children—all are contributing to a high level of frustration among the public as their daily lives and practices have been stalled without a clear idea about the future. A driver is vulnerable at any moment to a gunman forcing him or her out of the car. People are witnessing killings in public streets and in the middle of the day. Women are afraid to leave their houses for fear of rape and kidnapping. Mothers are afraid to let their kids walk to school on their own.

Impact on the Economy

Ambassador Paul Bremer's recent policy decree reinstating the distribution of salaries, including a great proportion of the former military's, is warmly welcomed by many Iraqis. Such steps are helpful to calm the immediate economic needs by those who were employed by the former government. The question now needs to extend to the private sector, including micro-, small- and medium-size enterprises. Such businesses have not been able to operate for more than 4 months now due to the lack of electricity and security. Small- and micro-businesses have been hardest hit, along with their employees who represent the most marginalized sectors of the population including women and single heads of households and others who are 100% dependent on these enterprises for their daily wages. Medium-size business losses are also impacting the business elite whose public support for Coalition forces is decreasing daily as their economic well being is further threatened.

The economy in general is veering from reliance on local production, particularly in areas related to food production, to an economy dependent more on processed and imported food. Addressing the revitalization of the local economy and local production is of the utmost importance in creating long term economic sustainability in Iraq. Lastly, most Iraqis, especially those who are poor and dependent on aid rations, constantly emphasized to me the need for economic security. A man who lives in a poor and old neighborhood of the Al Najef province, reflected to me on the current situation by saying: "We need food and security before democracy. When you save someone from death, his first wish is not a car but basic needs to regain his energy. The Americans, God bless them, are more concerned with democracy then they are addressing our basic needs." He continued, "We are a hungry population. Our need for food is more important than democracy at this point in our lives. That does not mean we don't want democracy. Rather, we need economic liberty as a prerequisite for democracy."

Impact on Women

Iraqi women are falling prey to the chaos and anarchy in Iraq. Women and girls are now targeted for kidnapping, with some women kidnapped from their own homes. Rumor, confirmed by coverage in *The Economist,* has it that there is now a market to sell women and girls in Baghdad. Women single heads of households are particularly vulnerable as movement outside of the home is becoming a risk for women because of the lack of security in the streets.

Politically, women's participation in discussions related to the national political agenda has been limited at best. Most local political parties do not actively encourage womens' participation. When this issue is addressed to local politicians, there seems to be no clear political agenda to exclude women as much as a lack of attention for the importance of women's participation in the political process.

Iraqi women, on the other hand, have been adamant about the importance of their political participation in the reconstruction of Iraq. Regardless of their socio-economic class, ethnic background, or religious or secular tendencies, all Iraqi women I met exhibited strong opinions on what is going on in today's Iraq and the need to incorporate them in the political process. Isma, a 40-year-old, woman who wears the traditional headscarf expressed her views on women to me by insisting that "I want Iraqi women to be part of every process of rebuilding the country ... in the army, in sport, in every single sector. Women need to have 50% representation in the country. I wish this could happen. We deserve that and we have the credibility to do that as well."

Addressing gender issues in the process of policy making, from the delivery of services to the establishment of a transitional governing body, is critical at this stage. Discussions related to promoting women's participation should not, however, be limited to one sector or channeled through one ministry. Rather, gender issues must be at the core of all reconstruction plans in Iraq. That includes but is not limited to strategies related to food distribution, police retraining, women's membership in political parties, and women's security in the public sphere. Otherwise, women will once again be marginalized in both the short and long term in Iraqi society. Women are also at risk from religious extremists. Some women who work with the UN have been threatened with death if they don't wear the traditional headscarf or quit working with "foreigners."

Political Parties

Local political parties, especially those who were based in exile, are showing no concrete efforts to address the concerns of the average citizen. "We have plenty of political parties but we don't have rule of law and we don't have work. So what is the use?" commented Ahmed who lives in Sadr City, a poor neighborhood in Baghdad.

There is a growing sense of a new political monopoly with economic overtones that is controlled by some of the parties that were based in exile and came in with the coalition forces and even those who were based in Iraqi Kurdistan. "Before we had one Saddam but now we have many mini Saddams who use power in similar ways as Saddam Hussein did," commented Ali, a businessman who describes himself as peace loving and a frustrated Iraqi. Now Iraqis feel that they must have an inside connection to those parties in order to gain access to information or services.

Most of these political parties, as well as the Coalition Provisional Authority, risk losing and alienating the average citizen by their lack of communication, transparency and clear political strategy. In commenting on this issue, Nashwan, a pharmacist who works in a public clinic in a poor neighborhood of Baghdad, said, "We want a leader with ethics, not a Ph.D." The Ph.D. is not the question here as much as a perceived lack of ethical and viable leadership from many of the political parties.

Lack of Information

Despite serious progress in addressing particular frustrations among Iraqis, including reinstating the distribution of salaries and food deliveries among others, there is a growing sense of anxiety regarding the future of Iraq. "We need to know what is going on. We need a public relations campaign that can speak to the concerns of the average Iraqi," comments Ahmed, a local Iraqi businessman who has not been able to run his business for four months now due to the lack of electricity.

The lack of information regarding not only the reinstallation of basic services but also the future of Iraq is creating a gap that is being filled by former Ba'athist officials on the one hand and religious extremists on the other. Former Ba'athist officials are taking advantage of the lack of information and services by spreading rumors that America doesn't care about Iraqis and the lack of services are intentional to keep Iraqis from contributing to the reformation process. There is a sense that former Ba'athist officials are regaining their ability to mobilize the public and spread anti-American sentiments. This can be seen in many ways including comments made by at least some in the police force about the greatness of the former regime in their daily communications with the public.

Religious extremists, on the other hand, are claiming that the lack of services is due to an imperial/Zionist conspiracy designed to destroy Iraq. The danger of these rumors is that they are speaking to the average Iraqi, especially male youth who have military training, are now unemployed, and are feeling a great level of frustration at the lack of stability in the country.

There are many ways to combat these rumors that are impacting the peace process in Iraq. Iraqis want to know what is happening in their country. A strong and consistent public relations campaign can keep Iraqis informed of future plans and engage them in the rebuilding process. "Iraqi public opinion is very very important. . . . Give us timelines so we know what is happening. Tell us what is the expected date for the complete reinstallation of the electricity and phone systems, when will there be a transitional Iraqi government, and how long the troops will stay here. We need information so at least we are not manipulated and frustrated by rumors," comments Dafir, a former government employee.

Ahmed, a businessman, reiterates the hunger for information by saying, "We need to know what is going on. We don't want to see soldiers killing two people every day or American soldiers being killed either. America needs to focus its communication to the average Iraqi . . . the real Iraqi . . . by helping them resume their daily work and daily life to a normal stage. Real people need to get a sense that America is communicating with them and addressing their concerns. If you lose the average person, you will lose the peace."

Conclusion

Iraqis are not only dealing with today's frustration, but also with the trauma caused by the oppression they have faced for 35 years during Ba'athist rule and particularly Saddam Hussein's regime. There is an outpouring of emotions in Iraq now which veer between frustration at the current chaos on the one hand and confronting the trauma and misery of the past for the first time in a public way—even within families—on the other. These emotions can be summarized by what one woman told me, as she described her life, "Every minute that passes, I die over and over again. I have already suffered a lot. I can't endure more suffering again." Iraqis are grateful to America for liberating them from Saddam Hussein, frustrated at America for not dealing with running the country the day after Saddam Hussein's collapse, and are now angry, tired, grateful, happy, and sad all at the same time. In other countries transitioning from a brutal period of civil strife, totalitarianism, or apartheid, truth and reconciliation commissions have gone a long way in acknowledging the pain and suffering caused to so many and allowed blame for crimes to be placed squarely on individuals and not ethnic groups, classes, or sects. There may be an opportunity here to not only allow Iraqis to heal many wounds but understand recent history, including the role played by organized violence against women.

One can also say that Iraqis have tremendous expectations from America, some that may be unrealistic in the time frame Iraqis are expecting. Many expect a Marshall Plan which will have an immediate impact within a few short months. Many are shocked at what is perceived to be limited preparation on how to manage a free Iraq. One Iraqi complained to me, questioning "How could the two most powerful countries in the world (the United States and the United Kingdom—who were able to win the war in one month) not have been prepared to deal with the day after the fall of Saddam Hussein's regime?". Others are now talking about starting think tanks to give advice to the Coalition Provisional Authority on how to run the country.

The frustrations that Iraqis are feeling today have many roots. Some stem from the perception that Iraqis are not being consulted in the process of policy formation on how to govern a free Iraq. Others feel that the lack of communication by coalition forces has left them vulnerable to rumors that only serve to increase their sense of anxiety about the future. And others feel that formerly exiled political parties are monopolizing all communication with the Coalition forces, reminding Iraqis of the former political structure known for its lack of transparency and corruption.

There are many ways in which Coalition forces under America's leadership can address frustrations at a grassroots level, building upon Amb. Bremer's accomplishments since his arrival in Iraq. First, and most important, there is a need for a massive public relations and communication campaign that goes beyond the two hours of Iraqi public TV that is running at the moment. Average Iraqis need to have their current challenges acknowledged, not whitewashed, and know that there is a public plan for dealing with these challenges. This will be the best way to directly combat the rumors being spread by forces opposed to the Coalition's role.

There is also a need to address the issue of expectations. Providing a timeline regarding the reinstallation of basic services, transitional government, and even economic plans can help in calming the situation down. There is a strong need to reach out to the hearts and minds of the average Iraqi by addressing real and immediate concerns he/she are facing and their anxiety about the future. Last but not least, we can win the peace in the Middle East in general, by adopting a policy of "Shock and Awe" for economic development in Iraq to match the overwhelming military superiority we brought to bear on the former regime. Such a policy will not only win the hearts and minds of the average Iraqi, it can also build credibility and support in neighboring countries and in the Middle East at large. I cannot conclude this testimony without emphasizing the importance of incorporating women throughout all governmental and non-governmental sectors and not limiting their participation to a single ministry or a single sector. Women are core participants in not only making peace but also in sustaining it.

Senator CORNYN. Thank you very much.

Senator FEINGOLD. Mr. Chairman, I just have a couple of unanimous consent——

Senator CORNYN. Sure. Senator Feingold.

Senator FEINGOLD. Mr. Chairman, Senator Kennedy asked that his statement be included in the record.

Senator CORNYN. Without objection.

STATEMENT SUBMITTED BY SENATOR EDWARD KENNEDY

Mr. Chairman, I commend you for arranging this joint hearing to consider the challenges we face in Iraq.

The major problem is that the war is supposed to be over, but it obviously isn't completely over. The daily attacks on our troops are very disturbing. Since President Bush landed on the aircraft carrier on May 1 and said "the war is over," our troops have continued to be killed at approximately half the rate as before.

The doubts that so many of us had about taking this road to war has only been strengthened by the failure so far to find the weapons of mass destruction that were the administration's principal justification for the war. And we are especially concerned by the suggestions that CIA intelligence reports were intentionally distorted by the White House or the Pentagon and turned into weapons of mass deceit.

Throughout this difficult period, all of us in Congress are united in support of the men and women of our Armed Forces, and we are committed to doing all we can to support them.

As the soldiers themselves have said, however, they aren't trained as police officers. We need to solve that problem as soon as possible. From past experience in Kosovo, Bosnia, and Afghanistan, we knew going into Iraq that we had to be prepared for the shift from war-fighting to peace-keeping to reconstruction and nation-building.

We rushed into this war, but it's obvious that winning the peace is much more challenging than the administration was prepared for. The "liberator" label has faded, and the "occupier" label is beginning to stick. The last thing we need is to alienate the Iraqi people after all we did to free them. The consequences would be ominous for the ongoing war against terrorism.

It's clear that we should do more to involve the United Nations and our allies in the reconstruction effort and in working with the Iraqi people to develop a new government. If we go it alone in creating a new government, the Iraqi people and nations around the world will see it as an American puppet government instead of a legitimate Iraqi government.

The bright spot is that the United Nations is carrying out its vital and historic role in meeting the humanitarian needs of the Iraqi people. The UN should be involved as well in the establishment of government institutions and civilian administration functions.

Above all, many of us are concerned about the ominous decline in respect for the United States in the eyes of so many other peoples and so many other nations caused, in large part, by our "shoot first and ask questions later" foreign policy. The breeding grounds of terrorism around the world are the only beneficiary of that decline. Unless we start getting it right in Iraq, we may well pay a very heavy cost for our failures.

So I look forward to this hearing and to working with our colleagues to do all we can to set a wiser course.

Senator FEINGOLD. And I ask unanimous consent that two documents be entered into the record as well: a report entitled, "Transitional Justice in Post-Saddam Iraq: The Road to Reestablishing Rule of Law and Restoring Civil Society," by the State Department Working Group on Transitional Justice and the Iraqi Jurists' Association; and a second document, "Iraq: Post-Conflict Justice, a Proposed Plan," by Professor M. Cherif Bassiouni, professor of law at the DePaul University College of Law.

Senator CORNYN. Without objection, those will be included.[1]

On May 22, the United Nations Security Council unanimously adopted a resolution, Number 1483, calling for the establishment of, "a representative government based on the rule of law that affords equal rights and justice to all Iraqi citizens without regard to ethnicity, religion, or gender."

It's been amazing to me really to see the number of people who have written and spoken expressing the view that there is somehow something inconsistent or incompatible about a nation where 95 percent of the people are Islamic, and democracy. I wonder if, Dr. Pollack, you could please start and just explain your view on that subject, whether you agree with that, or, as I suspect, you may disagree with that. Then what?

Dr. POLLACK. Thank you, Mr. Chairman. I will start. I think others on the panel would be equally if not more competent to deal with that question.

Let me start by saying first that there is nothing about any religion, as far as I am concerned, that has prohibition or injunction that would make it impossible to have a democratic form of government.

Too often when we start talking about democracy we allow our own individual associations, our own cultural associations with democracy to creep into that thought. I think when many Americans think about democracy, we have in mind American democracy. As someone who as traveled to many democratic countries over the course of my career, I'm always struck by how democracy looks very different in very different parts of the world.

As I mentioned in my opening remarks, Japan and Italy, to take only two examples, are also democracies, but Italian democracy and Japanese democracy are very different from our own. In fact, dealing with both of those systems, I sometimes wonder which is actually the democratic system. The fact of the matter is that democracy is rule by the people. That is its essence. If you go back to the Greek philosophers, if you go back to ancient Athens, that is the principle ingredient.

---

[1] The report "Transitional Justice in Post-Saddam Iraq: The Road to Reestablishing Rule of Law and Restoring Civil Society" appears in the appendix to this hearing; "Iraq: Post-Conflict Justice, a Proposed Plan," by Professor M. Cherif Bassiouni, can be found on the internet at http://www.law.depaul.edu/institutes centers/ihrli/pdf/iraq.pdf

When we talk about democracy in the modern sense, and when we talk about constitutions that are based on democracy, we're talking about some very basic principles. We're talking about a government that is reflective of the will of its people. We're talking about a government that is transparent, so that the people can monitor the actions of government officials to ensure that their actions are consistent with the will of the people, and we're talking about a system that is accountable in the sense that the officials themselves are ultimately accountable to the people for the actions that they take.

Those are really the heart of the democratic system and, in fact, the idea of the rule of law is embedded within that larger concept, because the idea of the rule of law is that the government should be of the people, it should not be oppressing any of the people, oppressing that which is ultimately the source of its legitimacy and its authority and power. There is nothing in Islam, as I read it and as I've read the work of my colleagues and of other colleagues, to indicate that there is anything in Islam that is incompatible with any of these basic precepts.

An Islamic democracy, an Arab democracy may look very different from ours, it may look very different from Japan's. It may look very different from Italy's, but there is nothing about the Koran, there is nothing about the Hadiths, there is nothing about Islam as it is practiced anywhere in the world that should make it incompatible with those basic fundamental premises.

Senator CORNYN. Thank you very much.

Professor Haykel and Dr. El Fadl, you both alluded to your belief that there should be an acknowledgement of Islam in the founding documents, the constitution of Iraq.

I found that to be interesting, in light of the fact that, as we may all recall, even in our Declaration of Independence there is an allusion to the Creator, and as my crack staff reminds me, even in the U.S. Constitution there is a reference to Our Lord, yet we do not seem to have too tough a problem separating our religious beliefs and practices from the secular work of government, but can you expand a little bit more on your belief of how the Iraqi people can address this notion of self-government and democracy and at the same time identify themselves as an Islamic nation, but not risk theocracy?

Professor Haykel, perhaps you'd like to start?

Dr. HAYKEL. You know, the question that you asked just earlier, Mr. Chairman, about the compatibility of Islamic democracy was asked at an earlier period in our own Nation's history about Catholics, with their allegiance to the Pope, and yet being Americans.

The thing to bear in mind about Islam, as in all religions, is that it's not a monolith. There are many different interpretations. There are many different ways of living and practicing Islam, and certainly there are strains within Islam that are theocratic and that would be anti-democratic, and we see them in bin Laden, we see them in certain strains of the Iranian clergy, but that's not to say that Islam cannot be lived in a democratic fashion, and we have good examples of that. Turkey is a perfect example of just that.

Even if we have allusion to religion and to Islam, Iraq is particularly a good example, I think, of a place where democracy can take root in a very strong way, because you have different types of Muslims in the country, as a result of which they would have to make accommodations to each other's differences and be cognizant of the fact that Islam is not a monolith and cannot impose their version on the others.

Senator CORNYN. Dr. El Fadl, do you agree or disagree?

Dr. EL FADL. No, I largely agree. I think the important distinction here is that I am not in a position to call upon the Iraqi people to mention Islam in the constitution. Rather, the distinction I make is that if the Iraqi people want to self-identify as Muslims, or make some mention of Islam in their foundational document, the U.S. Government should not oppose that and, more importantly, should not be threatened by that.

There are two things to keep in mind. One is that it is absolutely true that people, for all types of mischievous purposes and objectives, are trying to make it look as if what is going on now is a return of the colonial era, the era of imperialism, and that this is some type of war against Islam. I think it is essential that we do not make it easy for those people to win their dogmatic and propagandist war, and opposing all form of religious mention, or any form of Islamic self-identification would serve them well.

Second is that Bernard Haykel is absolutely right, there are many forms of Islam, some forms that are fundamentally inconsistent with democracy, but the core is as long as there is a commitment to individual rights, to the rights of an individual as an individual, and as long as the affirmation of an Islamic identity and the affirmation of Islamic preferences—we'd rather do X rather than Y because we believe one is closer to the Koran—as long as it's done in the context of honoring the basic truth of individual rights, it is reconcilable with democracy.

Senator CORNYN. Let me ask, Professor Haykel, I believe it was you that mentioned the concern about, during the de-Ba'athification process that there may be something in excess of 200,000 people in Iraq who, if forbidden to hold public jobs, would basically have very little option other than to create mischief for any nascent democracy. What do you propose, or what do you think should be our approach?

Dr. HAYKEL. Mr. Chairman, you know, government employment in the Middle East, whether it's in Iraq or elsewhere, is really—the governments are the main employers in the Middle East.

People look to government not in the way we do here, necessarily, because it is a major source of jobs, and in the Ba'ath period you have people who are committed Ba'athists who joined the party out of commitment, but most, or many did not. They joined it because that was how you got a job, and to penalize these people in some categorical fashion would mean penalizing not just them, but penalizing many, many members of their families who are dependent on them and on their connections with the government for jobs.

My fear really is that we would exclude 20 percent of the population from its source of revenue and livelihood, and that would cause tremendous social dislocation and political problems for us in the country.

Senator CORNYN. My time has expired.

Senator Chafee.

Senator CHAFEE. Thank you, Senator Cornyn. I'll follow-up on your questions about the possibility of a theocracy, and Professor Haykel, you doubted that that could happen. How do you base your confidence that a theocracy could not rise even if we allowed Islam into the constitution? Maybe just expand on that premise that you stated in your opening statement.

Dr. HAYKEL. It is alleged that 60 percent of the Iraqi population are Shiites. Now, the dominant theocratic model in Iran for the Shiites is that advocated by the late Imam Khomeini. Now, most Shiites, certainly in Iraq but also, it seems, in Iran don't support that constitutional model, the constitutional model he advocated.

My assertion is based on knowledge that the Shiites of Iraq are very different from those in Iran, that the Iranian model is not necessarily applicable and is not accepted by a great number of the clerics in Iraq, who tend to be more quietist in their political position.

Senator CHAFEE. And Ms. Salbi, you've just returned from Iraq, and I see you nodding your head. Do you agree with that, that—it was a couple of weeks ago I believe there were some clerics who I believe issued a declaration of Jihad against the occupying forces. Is this taking hold with the population?

Ms. SALBI. First, I have to reiterate what Professor Haykel said. The premise of Shiism is the separation of religion from the state. Khomeini was the only person in Shiite history who combined the state with religion. Iraq Shias so very much believe in the separation of the State and religion.

The fear is not from the learned unama, because they're learned—I mean, they descended over 15 to 20 years on religious jurisprudence and all of that. The fear is from the younger ones, young men in their twenties who have religious tendencies, like Moktar el Sadr, who is approaching other men who are released from the army, former Republican Guard, and then mobilizing their anger and frustration at the current economic situation for religious reasons. That's the fear.

That's still a minority group. They're still approaching the youth. They're not approaching the middle-aged people, or the learned people, but that could be a gap that could be widened if we do not address the immediate economic needs right now, so that's one thing that you can see the beginning of it.

In general, when you talk to all the Iraqis, whether in the south or in the center, they do want a secular government. They do not say we want a secular government per se, but they say, we want a civil government that respects Islam as a religion, we want civil law that regulates the country, and that is people from conservative to secular people, and they're all saying that. It's a very emotional feeling that we need to respect Islam, and a very emotional feeling that we need a civil law to regulate our country.

Senator CHAFEE. With this catching on with the younger people, is it directed at Americans, or is it the coalition, British—would it be better if the United Nations were more involved in this process and remove the prospect that it's an American issue here?

Ms. SALBI. I have to say, there is no public sentiment that sympathizes with the U.N. in Iraq. The U.N. was accused of being part of the previous regime's corruption scandals and scams, and so the U.N. is not necessarily viewed in the best way.

These religious sentiments, having said that, they are directing that anger at the Americans. I wrote in my report, a lot of the religious sentiments is trying to approach, again to deal with that economic urgent gap by saying, this is an American-Zionist conspiracy aimed at destroying Iraq, while the Ba'athists are also trying to fill that gap by saying America is intending to keep the Iraqis frustrated, to keep them away from the political process.

So we are vulnerable now to these groups, again, taking advantage of these gaps and in my opinion, my assessment by talking to people is that we can actually win that easy if we just address the immediate and urgent needs by the Iraqis and stabilize the economic and security conditions right now.

Senator CHAFEE. Thank you. You do have a prescription for success, and that's relevant to a Marshall Plan-type of restoration of the country.

Thank you, Mr. Chairman.

Senator CORNYN. Senator Feingold.

Senator FEINGOLD. Thank you, Mr. Chairman.

Dr. El Fadl, Professor Haykel, and Mr. Al-Sarraf, we've heard testimony today about the strong legacy of legal thought and legal institutions that existed before the Ba'ath Party took power in 1968 and then, of course, the damage done under Saddam's regime.

I'd like each of you to comment on whether that legacy survived in any form, to what extent will the Iraqi people be able to look back on their own legal traditions and effectively draw upon that experience as they reconstruct their nation and its institutions.

Let's start with Dr. El Fadl again.

Dr. EL FADL. Well, I think it's important here to keep in mind the complexity and nuance of law, because if you take, for instance, the civil law code, which was derived from the French civil code, and in fact borrowed extensively from the Egyptian work on the French civil code and, in the view of some, even improved upon from the Egyptian version, you take the Iraqi civil code and the jurisprudence that formed around the civil code in Iraq, similarly if you exclude the literal, the shameful displays committed by Saddam in order to get attention and so on, if you take the criminal law code, exclude all the Saddam exceptional laws and emergency laws and special laws and just take the criminal code and the jurisprudence formed around the criminal code, what you find is actually something that from a legal perspective is quite sophisticated, belongs in the best of the tradition of the civil law system based on the French legal system, something in which, for instance, in the civil law field and in the criminal law field some of the works of Egyptian jurists like Sanhouri, one of the most prominent jurists who is dead now—he was cited extensively and worked with and developed upon and so on—you actually find, a lot of commonality between the technical jurisprudence of Iraq and the jurisprudence of particularly countries like Egypt, to a lesser extent countries like Kuwait.

Second is that you find a large degree of technical sophistication, and in fact, in working with Iraqi lawyers, the complaint was consistently that the Saddam regime ruined the practice of law, that unlike their Egyptian counterparts, for instance, they could not say that they follow X school of thought as to personal injuries because they were always scared that Saddam was going to come in with some exceptional law, some special regulation and so on.

The best way that I think the issue can be approached is to realize that we have a substantial amount of very sophisticated jurisprudence, that it is possible, in my opinion, to peel off the Saddam special laws, special regulations, special this and that, and to work from that, rather than reinvent the wheel, and try to create some type of revolutionary law which is fraught with possibilities of failure.

Senator FEINGOLD. Thank you very much. Professor Haykel.

Dr. HAYKEL. I would like to reiterate and second what Professor Abou El Fadl just said. As someone who actually has followed the production, the legal, intellectual production from Iraqi universities even through the Saddam period, the University in Baghdad, for example, had a couple of legal journals, one from the university, one from the ministry of justice, and they consistently had very high quality legal thought and legal academic production.

With respect to the period before Saddam Hussein, I mean, there are documents, legal documents that still exist and that can be drawn upon, and also in the collective memory, I think, of Iraqis, especially the period in the twenties, when there was a very vibrant Jewish community in Iraq, perhaps the most vibrant Jewish community in the Arab world, that period again is something that Iraqis remember as a time when Iraq really was the center of the Arab world, and where you had pluralism and a great degree of tolerance.

I think that period can be revised very quickly, because you have a very high technical cadre of people in Iraq who are middle class but also very educated, I think for whom this period really is something they hark back to and wish to recreate today.

Senator FEINGOLD. Thank you. Mr. Al-Sarraf.

Mr. AL-SARRAF. Thank you. It's important to note how Saddam subordinated the judiciary. The judiciary basically used to report to an independent judicial authority. That judicial authority was then placed under the Ministry of Justice and became part of the executive.

Then what Saddam did is, he created special courts in the Ministry of Information, the Ministry of the Interior under the security forces, the military had their own courts, the police had their own courts, so basically every court system reported to an executive who had the final say.

The Ministry of Justice, however, dealt primarily with just civil and criminal affairs and was left largely intact, except for when Ba'ath Party members were involved, so what you have are individuals that work in the Ministry of Justice, and I had the opportunity in the last few days to meet with the interim Minister of Justice who arrived in New York a few days ago and is addressing the United Nations, and it's individuals like him who understand from the inside—he's been with the judiciary for 43 years, understands it inside and out, and has an idea of how to reform, and it requires a vetting process. It's a long-term process.

There's also a cadre of forcibly retired jurists, those who would not go along with the Ba'ath Party rule, who also represent a constituency or a resource within the country, so the first premise is that it has to be rebuilt from the inside, and the second is that there can be international assistance, but we have to be very careful about who those international experts are, because there is sensitivity inside the country about who they will work with.

Senator FEINGOLD. Thank you.

Dr. Pollack, you suggested that international involvement might be helpful in giving legitimacy to the constitutional process. What do you see as the role of the United Nations and the international community in drafting an Iraqi constitution? Would you suggest, for example, that the United States ask the United Nations, or a third country, to take over leadership of the constitutional process?

Dr. POLLACK. Thank you, Senator. No, I would not suggest that. I think that the constitutional process must be led by Iraqis. That said, I think that all of these international organizations, and I think that all the members of the coalition, the increasingly expanding coalition, have important roles to play within that.

First, the transitional authority itself will have a role in literally setting up a constitutional commission of some sort. They will have to take care of the administrative side of things. On that issue, as on all matters, as far as I'm concerned, the more the United States can work in conjunction with the United Nations, now that we have Sergio de Mello as the new Special Representative of the Secretary General, someone who's very skilled in these kind of operations, a good partner for Paul Bremer, I think that it is incumbent upon us to work in conjunction with them to indicate that this is not a U.S.-only operation.

Senator FEINGOLD. The thrust of my question was, wouldn't it better, or arguable that we should turn over this responsibility of helping, the leadership role, to another country, rather than doing it ourselves?

Dr. POLLACK. Again, I would not suggest that we necessarily turn it over to another country. I certainly think that we should be involving as many countries as we possibly can. I think that the United States at the end of the day has a responsibility to make sure that Iraq is a stable, functional society when the international occupation has ended. We're the ones who started this. We're the ones who have got to make sure that it succeeds.

That said, I also don't think that the United States should necessarily be directing the Iraqis to do this, that or the other thing. I just think it ought to be a joint effort, not any one country.

Senator FEINGOLD. I'm going to take this to Ms. Salbi now, because I want to know her thoughts on the issue of international involvement with regard to my question to Dr. Pollack, but also based on your experience in other post-conflict societies like Afghanistan and Kosovo.

Ms. SALBI. Two things. One is, we need to acknowledge the high level of frustration that has been built in Iraq for 35 years. What the Iraqis are going through is that for the first time in their history, or in 35 years, they can talk about Saddam's oppression, so a Truth and Reconciliation Committee would be something that would be very helpful in just at least processing these frustrations and the injustices that they have been through, and acknowledging them at a minimum.

The second thing, when I talked to local political parties over there, and I was talking to them about different models and different experiences, from Afghanistan to South Africa, there was a hunger for information. Remember, Iraqis have been blocked from any information outside of Iraq, and everyone was eager to know, what is the South African constitution, what are the pros and cons of the Afghan reconstruction process, and so I do think that it has to have a local ownership, but that process needs to inform them and to share information from different countries.

South Africa is a great model, Afghanistan is a good model to look at, with Iraqi leadership, with our support, making sure that we're feeding the Iraqis all in the information in the process.

Senator FEINGOLD. But is it better for the United States to be perceived as taking the lead outside role, or would it be better if the United Nations—and I know you expressed strong reservations about the United Nations—or a third country were in that role in that context?

Ms. SALBI. I personally don't have reservations about the United States as much as the Iraqis do. I think the Iraqis are looking for America's leadership, but they are looking also at America's communication, and they want to be incorporated in the process, and there is a sense that they are cutoff from whatever process that is going on in dealing with Iraq.

So the majority of the sentiments is still, people are looking for America. It's just that they are frustrated, that they don't think America is reaching out to them.

Senator FEINGOLD. Thank you very much.

Thank you, Mr. Chairman.

Senator CORNYN. Thank you, Senator Feingold. I'd like to express my gratitude, and I know I speak for all of us here, at your participation, the members of the first panel.

Oh, I beg your pardon. Senator Chafee has another question or two.

Senator CHAFEE. Just before we give our thanks to this panel, Ms. Salbi, since you were just in Iraq, do the Iraqi people think that Saddam Hussein is still alive? Do they think that, and is that significant?

Ms. SALBI. I am glad you asked this question. Yes, they do think that he is alive. His family members are moving very freely, actually in the streets of Iraq, not only female family members, which we could argue it's safer for them, but male family members, his cousins, his nephews, who are notorious for their oppression and violence during this regime, so there is not only a sentiment that he is still in Iraq, but the Ba'athists are also being relaxed about the security issue, that they are feeling comfortable to walk the streets of Iraq, especially in the evenings and at nights.

Senator CHAFEE. And how big an issue is that as we go forward?

Ms. SALBI. Again, we can contain that because what's happening is that there are gaps of information and the Ba'athists are taking advantage of these gaps, as are the religious extremists, but particularly the Ba'athists by saying, look, Saddam was better for us than the Americans.

When you ask the police force if they are happy now Saddam is out, some say no, they wish Saddam were back. A lot of former employees are returning, and they should return because they need the jobs and we need to stabilize the economy, but we really need to reeducate them and retrain them as to what the former regime has done and what their role should be in the future.

Senator CHAFEE. Very good. Thank you.

Senator CORNYN. Thank you, Senator Chafee, and thanks to each of you on the first panel. I'll just remind everybody that we're going to leave the record open until July 2 in case any other member of the joint subcommittees would like to submit any further questions, or if there any other documents that you'd like to offer in support of your testimony in this record, we would invite you to do so. Thank you very much.

Now I'd like to invite the members of the second panel to come forward, a panel of distinguished constitutional legal experts; while they take their seats I will introduce them.

First, we're happy to have Professor John Yoo here. Professor Yoo served as Deputy Attorney General for the Office of Legal Counsel at the U.S. Department of Justice from 2001 until just last month. In that role, he served in the Bush administration as one of its top legal advisors in the war on terrorism and the war on Iraq. He's a nationally recognized expert in international law, U.S. constitutional law, and national security and foreign relations law.

Professor Naoyuki Agawa is a recognized expert on both the Japanese and the United States constitutions. He served as a professor at the University of Virginia Law School, Georgetown Law School and Keio University. He holds bar memberships in both the United States and Japan, and has practiced law in both Washington, D.C. and Tokyo.

Dr. Donald Kommers is a recognized expert on the German constitution. He is both the Joseph and Elizabeth Robbie professor of Political Studies at Notre Dame and a law professor at Notre Dame Law School. He's authored 10 books and 67 articles primarily in the area of American, German and comparative law and German politics.

Our fifth panel member is Professor Dick Howard, who is the White Burkett Miller Professor of Law and Public Affairs at the University of Virginia Law School, where he and I first had an opportunity to meet. Professor Howard is an expert in constitutional law and comparative constitutionalism. Numerous countries have sought his counsel in the process of drafting their constitutions, including Brazil, Hong Kong, the Philippines, Hungary, Czechoslovakia, Poland, Romania, Russia, Albania, South Africa, and India, quite an impressive list.

I know we have Mr. Neil Kritz, who is director of the Rule of Law program at the United States Institute of Peace. That program focuses on advancing peace through the development of democratic, legal, and governmental systems, precisely the topic we have before us here today. He is the editor of a three-volume work called "Transitional Justice: How Emerging Democracies Reckon with Former Regimes," and I imagine has quite a bit to offer on the subject before us today.

I want to thank each one of you for being here, and your patience. Now we'd like to hear from each of you, if we might, and if you would please keep your opening statement to 5 minutes, then we'll proceed to questions.

Professor Yoo.

STATEMENT OF JOHN YOO, VISITING FELLOW, AMERICAN ENTERPRISE INSTITUTE

Mr. YOO. Thank you, Mr. Chairman, Chairman Chafee, thank you for inviting me to appear, and I'd like to compliment you and your committee on your leadership in holding hearings on this important topic, which I think will be central to guaranteeing the future and long-term stability of Iraq.

I would also just like to make clear that the views expressed here are my own, and not those of the American Enterprise Institute or the University of California, Berkeley.

I think my point of view here is that of a lawyer, in that I can tell you what you can do, but I can't tell you what you should do, and in that capacity I'd like to point to three sources of law that give the United States the authority, as the occupying power in Iraq, to establish a constitution that guarantees basic, individual human rights and that operates within a rule of law with democratic representative institutions.

The first is our own domestic constitution. Iraq is not the first country that the United States has occupied, and the Supreme Court in several cases has examined the question of occupation and has stated quite clearly that occupation includes the power to change laws and constitutions of the territory that is occupied because it is part of the war power.

We're still in a state where legally the state of armed conflict continues to exist in Iraq and does not terminate until a peace treaty has been signed, and as part of the effort to wage a successful campaign that may include eliminating aspects of the local governmental system that pose a threat, continue to pose a threat to peace and stability and to the United States and the region.

Here in Iraq, the second major source of authority comes from the United Nations. There are two separate resolutions that bear on the question of occupation. First is the resolution passed in 1991, Resolution 678, which originally authorized all member nations to use all necessary means, quote-unquote, to remove Iraq from Kuwait, to enforce other relevant resolutions, and to restore international peace and security to the region.

One of those significant resolutions was to eliminate WMD in Iraq. Another resolution is to prevent Iraq's regime from terrorizing its own civilian population. That resolution, number 678, ultimately was one of the sources of authority for the war in Iraq. Also, by requiring that member nations restore international peace and security, to the extent that the Iraqi constitution as it was, and the Saddam Hussein regime encouraged or enabled a specific regime to continue to pose a threat to that region, then obviously Resolution 678 could be used also to eliminate the legal aspects of that threat.

The second and more recent actions of the Security Council came, as you mentioned in your opening statement, in Resolution 1483, which was passed just a few weeks ago. In that resolution, the United Nations Security Council recognized the United States and Great Britain as occupying powers in Iraq. It expressed its hope that the Iraqis would be encouraged to establish a representative government with protection for human rights and the rule of law, and also stated that the United States and Great Britain would be subject to their obligations under what's known as the Hague Regulations and the Geneva Conventions, which are primary treaties in the area of occupation.

Just to turn to that last point, then, the third source of authority for America's ability to establish a constitution for Iraq that is based on the rule of law and democratic institutions comes from those two basic treaties, the Hague Regulations of 1907, and the Fourth Geneva Convention of 1949.

The Hague Regulation of 1907, Article 43, allows an occupying power to change the domestic laws of the country that is occupied if it is necessary to restore public order and safety, so again in this case, as I think the first panel discussed, a lot of the negative aspects of Saddam Hussein's regime were actually incorporated and codified into the legal system and into the constitution, so to the extent that the Hussein regime and its instruments were the basic threat to order and security in its own country, removal of those constitutional provisions and those statutes would be justified under the Hague Regulations.

The second point is, Iraq isn't even a signatory to the Hague Regulations, so to the extent the Hague Regulations are more of a customary international law, then the interpretations that countries have put up on it in their State practice would be more important, and here I defer to my other panel members, but the experiences in Germany and Japan in particular show how States have interpreted Article 43 of the Hague Regulation. In both of those examples, obviously, the United States exercised a great deal of discretion and authority in encouraging a certain kind of constitution for Germany and Japan.

And just a last point, the last source of authority is the Fourth Geneva Convention, which is much more liberal, I suppose you could say, in its grant of authority to an occupying power. Article 64 of the Fourth Geneva Convention says that the occupying power may subject the population of the occupied territory to provisions which are essential to enable the occupying power to fulfill its obligations under the present convention, by which it means basic human rights, to maintain the orderly government of the territory, and to assure the security of the occupying power.

Article 64 of the Geneva Convention, therefore, would provide a legal basis for the United States in Iraq to institute and establish changes to the Iraqi constitution and its legal system consistent with achieving basic human rights, protecting safety and security, and protecting the United States' own security interests.

Thank you, Mr. Chairman.

[The prepared statement of Mr. Yoo follows:]

PREPARED STATEMENT OF JOHN YOO

Mr. Chairman, thank you for the opportunity to appear before your committee today to discuss the reconstruction of Iraq and its constitution. I wish to complement you and the committee for convening today's hearings on this important subject, which will be critical to providing for Iraq's long-term stability and ensuring that Iraq will become a law-abiding member of the international community. Rather than discuss any specific element of a proposed Iraqi constitution, I appear before you today to discuss the authority of the United States, under domestic and international law, to make fundamental changes to the constitutional law and government institutions of Iraq. I conclude that United Nations Security Council resolutions and the international law of occupation provide the United States with broad discretion to establish a new Iraq constitution, one that guarantees fundamental human rights protected by democratic institutions that limit government power.

I have studied these issues for much of my career. I recently left the Department of Justice, where I served as Deputy Assistant Attorney General in the Office of Legal Counsel (OLC). OLC advises the executive branch on all legal questions, including those involving treaties and international law. I am currently a visiting fellow at the American Enterprise Institute, and a professor of law at the University of California at Berkeley School of Law (Boalt Hall), where I have taught foreign affairs law, international law, and constitutional law, since 1993. It was also my great honor to have served as General Counsel of the Senate Judiciary Committee under Chairman Hatch from 1995–96. I wish to make clear that the views expressed here are my own, and do not represent those of the American Enterprise Institute or the University of California.

I. DOMESTIC LAW AND OCCUPATION

Under our domestic law, occupation of a nation is merely the continuation of hostilities, and thus the reconstruction of Iraq falls within the war powers of the federal government. Occupying foreign territory during the transition period between an armed conflict and a declaration of peace, and establishing fundamental institutional changes to the government of an enemy nation, may be essential to reaching a successful conclusion to war. If allowed to remain in existence, the institutions of an occupied nation may continue to pose a threat to the safety of U.S. troops or the national security. Or the government institutions of the defeated enemy have been so degraded or destroyed that they cannot provide security and basic services to the local population. If left to suffer, a local population may become hostile to the United States. To be fully successful, military operations in an occupied territory may have to continue even as the immediate need for force has subsided.

In several previous armed conflicts, the United States has exercised its authority to occupy and govern a foreign nation after a successful military campaign. The Supreme Court has clearly upheld this authority. In *MacLeod* v. *United States,* for example, which arose during the U.S. military occupation of the Philippines during the Spanish-American War, a unanimous Supreme Court explained that

> [t]he right to ... occupy an enemy's country and temporarily provide for its government has been recognized by previous action of the executive authority, and sanctioned by frequent decisions of this court. The local government being destroyed, the conqueror may set up its own authority, and make rules and regulations for the conduct of temporary government, and to that end may collect taxes and duties to support the military authority and carry on operations incident to the occupation.[1]

The Court similarly stated with respect to the U.S. occupation of Puerto Rico that

> [u]pon the occupation of the country by the military forces of the United States, the authority of the Spanish Government was superseded ... The government must be carried on, and there was no one left to administer its functions but the military forces of the United States. ... The right of one belligerent to occupy and govern the territory of the enemy while in its military possession, is one of the incidents of war, and flows directly from the right to conquer. We, therefore, do not look to the Constitution or political institutions of the conqueror, for authority to establish a government for the territory of the enemy in his possession, during its military occupation, nor for the rules by which the powers of such government are regulated and limited. Such authority and such rules are derived directly from the laws of war, as established by the usage of the world, and confirmed by the writings of publicists and decisions of courts—in fine, from the law of the nations.[2]

---

[1] 229 U.S. 416, 425 (1913).
[2] *Dooley,* 182 U.S. at 230–31 (quoting 2 Halleck, *International Law,* 444).

As the Supreme Court has further made clear, the power to establish an occupation government and to make decisions concerning reconstruction flow directly from the President's Commander-in-Chief power.[3]

It is not difficult to see why occupation and reconstruction of a defeated enemy may be an important aspect of the war power. Eliminating a threat to the national security or achieving U.S. foreign policy goals may not only require the occupation of an enemy nation until its capacity to attack the United States has ended, but also the extensive reordering of an occupied nation's domestic institutions. Replacing a hostile government with new institutions may make the defeated nation less of a threat to the United States, both now and in the future, and may end human rights abuses. At the end of World War H, the United States not only occupied part of Germany, it completely refashioned, along with the other Allied powers, German government institutions. The United States believed that preventing Germany from "ever again becoming a threat to the peace of the world" would require "the elimination of Nazism and militarism in all their forms, the immediate apprehension of war criminals for punishment, the industrial disarmament and demilitarization of Germany, with continuing control over Germany's capacity to make war, and the preparation for an eventual reconstruction of German political life on a democratic basis."[4] Similarly, the United States also reordered the Government of Japan following the conclusion of World War II, although these changes, unlike those in Germany, were carried out with the consent of the Japanese Government. Again, the rationale underlying this fundamental government reform was to guarantee that Japan would not again become a military threat to the United States or the world.[5]

II. INTERNATIONAL LAW AND OCCUPATION

International law authorizes a victorious nation both to establish its own temporary occupation government and to make changes in the laws of the defeated nation prior to the conclusion of a treaty of peace. This authority includes the power to make fundamental institutional changes to the government of an occupied nation. Here, I will address the sources of law that establish the authority of the United States, as an occupying power, to replace the forms of the previous Hussein regime with new governmental institutions and a new constitution. These sources include Security Council Resolutions under Chapter VII of the United Nations Charter, which gives the Council the authority to bind member nations, and the international law of occupation as expressed in treaties and state practice.

United Nations Authorization

The United States has been authorized by the Security Council to occupy Iraq and, as a consequence, to establish a constitution and form of government that will end the threat posed by the Hussein regime to international peace and security. This authority comes from two sources, the original 1991 authorization to use force against Iraq (S.C. Res 678), and the recent May, 2003 Security Council resolution approving the occupation of Iraq at the end of major combat operations in Iraq (S.C. Res. 1483).

In 1991, the Security Council enacted a resolution that recognized the legitimacy of the U.S.-led international coalition's use of military force against Iraq. Security Council resolution 678 explicitly recognized that member states could "use all necessary means" (1) to respond to the Iraqi regime's substantial violations of the terms of the cease-fire set forth in UNSCR 687 that suspended hostilities between Iraq and a U.S.-led international coalition in 1991; and (2) to restore international peace and security in the area. In particular, Iraq had flagrantly breached its various obligations under UNSCR 687 regarding the destruction and dismantling, under international supervision, of its weapons of mass destruction ("WMD") programs. The Security Council itself decided last year that Iraq "has been and remains in material

---

[3] *See, e.g., Madsen* v. *Kinsella,* 343 U.S. 341, 348 (1952) ("[t]he President has the urgent and infinite responsibility not only of combating the enemy but of governing any territory occupied by the United States by force of arms."); *Fleming* v. *Page,* 50 U.S. (9 How.) 603 (1850) (power to occupy captured territory is "simply that of a military commander prosecuting a war waged against a public enemy by the authority of his government."); *Hirota* v. *MacArthur,* 338 U.S. 197, 208 (1948) (Douglas, J., concurring) ("[The President's] power as Commander in Chief is vastly greater than that of troop commander. He not only has full power to repel and defeat the enemy; he has the power to occupy the conquered country ... ").

[4] Directive to Commander in Chief of United States Forces of Occupation Regarding the Military Government of Germany, (Apr. 1945), *reprinted in* "The Axis in Defeat: A Collection of Documents on American Policy Toward Germany and Japan," 43–44, (1945).

[5] *See* U.S. Initial Post-Surrender Policy for Japan, (Aug. 29, 1945), *reprinted in* "The Axis in Defeat: A Collection of Documents on American Policy Toward Germany and Japan," (setting forth objectives for post-World War II occupation of Japan), 107, (1945).

breach of its obligations under relevant resolutions, including resolution 687" as a result of its failure to comply with its disarmament obligations.[6] in the same resolution, the Security Council also recalled that those obligations imposed upon Iraq under UNSCR 687 constituted "a necessary step for achievement of UNSCR 687's stated objective of restoring international peace and security in the area."

The Security Council's authorization to "use all necessary means" to disarm Iraq and to restore international peace and security in the area includes not only the use of force but also the subsequent occupation. An occupation of Iraq is necessary to locate, catalog, dismantle, and destroy all Iraqi WMD programs and thus ensure that Iraq is in compliance with UNSCR 687. Given the lengths to which the Hussein regime has gone to conceal its WMD programs and the years it has had to hide its arms, the United States cannot rid Iraq of its WMD programs during the course of major combat operations. In addition, were the United States and its coalition partners to depart from Iraq immediately following the end of combat, the peace and security of the region might be threatened. Violence could erupt among Iraq's various ethnic and religious groups that could spill beyond Iraq's borders. Iraq could descend into a state of anarchy. Such a development would not only threaten Iraq's neighbors but also could turn Iraq into a haven for terrorist organizations. A humanitarian crisis could also result from political turmoil, leading to a flood of refugees entering and destabilizing Iraq's neighbors. Remnants of the current Iraq regime could seek to reconstitute themselves, which would pose a threat to Iraq's neighbors. To fulfill the goals of U.N. Security Council Resolution 678, the United States must occupy Iraq, establish an interim administration, and construct stable Iraqi government institutions that will help to restore peace and security to the region.

The U.S.'s authority to occupy Iraq is confirmed by Resolution 1483, which was adopted by the Security Council on May 22, 2003 by a unanimous vote (with Syria not voting). in that resolution, the Security Council recognized the United States and Great Britain as the "occupying powers" in Iraq, and it encouraged "efforts by the people of Iraq to form a representative government based on the rule of law that affords equal rights and justice to all Iraqi citizens without regard to ethnicity, religion, or gender." The Security Council resolved "that the United Nations should play a vital role in humanitarian relief, the reconstruction of Iraq, and the restoration and establishment of national and local institutions for representative governance." It also called upon the United States and Great Britain "consistent with the Charter of the United Nations and other relevant international law, to promote the welfare of the Iraqi people through the effective administration of the territory, including in particular working toward the restoration of conditions of security and stability and the creation of conditions in which the Iraqi people can freely determine their own political future." In addition to approving the financial arrangements for the sale of Iraqi oil and the use of the proceeds, Resolution 1483 "calls upon all concerned to comply fully with their obligations under international law including in particular the Geneva Conventions of 1949 and the Hague Regulations of 1907."

I will review the authority provided by the Geneva Conventions and the Hague Regulations shortly. It is important, however, to understand that by making clear that the two treaties apply to the occupation of Iraq, the Security Council has explicitly recognized that the United States may exercise the broad authorities granted by those conventions. Further, Resolution 1483 expresses the Security Council's hope that Iraq will reform its government in order to establish representative institutions subject to the rule of law and protection for human rights. The Security Council, however, did not detail the specific authorities that would empower the United States and its allies to move Iraq toward a constitution with democratic institutions. Therefore, the power to achieve these goals must flow from the existing international law of occupation, as expressed in state practice and applicable treaties. These sources allow the occupying powers, here the United States and Great Britain, to alter the domestic laws, including the constitution and government institutions, in order to provide for stability and security in Iraq, to protect the basic human rights of Iraqis, and to restore international peace and security in the region.

Customary Law and the Hague Regulations

The laws of war govern the conduct of warfare by and between states. This body of law is both reflected in the customary practice of nations and codified in various texts, including the Hague Convention (IV) Respecting the Laws and Customs of War on Land, Oct. 18, 1907, 36 Stat. 2277 ("Hague Convention") and the Geneva

[6] S.C. Res. 1441, ¶ 1 (2002). See also S.C. Res. 707, ¶ 1 (1991); S.C. Res. 1137, ¶ 1 (1997); S.C. Res. 1205, ¶ 1 (1998).

Conventions. The laws of war recognize that, as the result of armed conflict, any surviving elements of the enemy nation may be incapable of providing public services and maintaining security. Additionally, victorious armies have sought to control enemy territory in order to deprive the enemy of valuable resources and to produce surrender. The laws of war thus include a specific set of rules to govern the conduct of military occupations and the operation of military government. This international law of occupation not only authorizes a victorious nation to occupy enemy territory and establish a military government; it also recognizes the authority of an occupant to change the local laws, including government institutions.

Because the international law of occupation is partially formed, by custom and practice, and, as will be explained below, the central treaty on occupation does not apply to Iraq, it is important to review the historical development of the legal rules in this area. Historically, an occupying army enjoyed wide discretion in administering the territory of a defeated enemy.[7] An occupant was generally considered the permanent and absolute owner of occupied territory. Since the nineteenth century, however, the law has understood the occupying authority to exercise only temporary control over territory. Permanent control would result only from a treaty of peace concluded at the end of a military conflict or the complete subjugation of an enemy.[8] The first efforts to codify the laws of war, and more specifically the law of occupation, began in the United States during the Civil War. In 1862, the War Department commissioned the drafting of a set of basic instructions for Union soldiers on the law of war. Approximately one-third of the resulting General Order No. 100, also known as the "Lieber Code," addressed rules relating to occupation. The Lieber Code explained that "[a] place, district, or country occupied by an enemy stands, in consequence of the occupation, under the martial law of the invading or occupying army, whether any proclamation declaring martial law, or any public warning to the inhabitants has been issued or not."[9]

The institution of martial law, in turn, provided an occupant with the authority both to suspend the laws of an occupied nation and to subject the population of an occupied nation to new laws. The Lieber Code provided, "Martial law in a hostile country consists in the suspension by the occupying military authority of the criminal and civil law, and of the domestic administration and government in the occupied place or territory, and in the substitution of military rule and force for the same, as well as in the dictation of general laws, as far as military necessity requires this suspension, substitution, or dictation."[10] The scope of the occupant's authority to suspend, substitute, or dictate the law of the occupied territory was quite broad, due to the Lieber Code's broad definition of the concept of military necessity."[11]

International efforts to codify the laws of war followed. The 1874 Brussels Declaration, although not a legally binding agreement, specifically authorized the conduct of military occupation, stating that "[t]he authority of the legitimate power being suspended and having in fact passed into the hands of the occupant, the latter shall take all the measures in his power to restore and ensure, as far as possible, public order and safety."[12] Like the Lieber Code, the Brussels Declaration expressly recognized the authority of occupants to change the laws of the indigenous government in certain situations: "With this object he shall maintain the laws which were in force in the country in time of peace and shall not modify, suspend or replace them by others unless necessary."[13] Although the Brussels Declaration established a presumption in favor of "maintain[ing] the laws which were in force in the country

---

[7] *See* Doris A. Graber, *The Development of the Law of Belligerent Occupation 1863–1914,* at 13, (1949).

[8] *See* 3 Emmerich de Vattel, *The Law of Nations or The Principles of Natural Law, Applied to the Conduct and to the Affairs of Nations and of Sovereigns,* 308, (Charles G. Fenwick, trans., 1916), (1758) ("Real property—lands, towns, provinces—become the property of the enemy who takes possession of them; but it is only by the treaty of peace; or by the entire subjection and extinction of the State to which those towns and provinces belong, that the acquisition is completed and ownership rendered permanent and absolute."); *American Ins. Co.* v. *Canter,* 26 U.S. (1 Pet.) 511, 542 (1828) ("[T]he usage of the world is, if a nation be not entirely subdued, to consider the holding of conquered territory as a mere military occupation, until its fate shall be determined at the treaty of peace.").

[9] General Order No. 100, section I, ¶ 1.

[10] General Order No. 100, section I, ¶ 3.

[11] General Order No. 100, section I, ¶ 14 (defining "[m]ilitary necessity" as "consist[ing] in the necessity of those measures which are indispensable for securing the ends of the war, and which are lawful according to the modern law and usages of war").

[12] Draft of an International Declaration concerning the Laws and Customs of War adopted by the Conference of Brussels, August, 27, 1874, art. 2.

[13] Id. art. 3.

in time of peace," it also allowed the occupant to "modify, suspend or replace" those laws when necessity required.

The Brussels Declaration became the basis for the Hague Conventions of 1899 and 1907. The Hague Conventions acknowledged both the legality of military occupation and the authority of occupants to change indigenous laws and institutions. Article 42 of the Hague Convention of 1907, known as the "Hague Regulations," states that "[t]erritory is considered occupied when it is actually placed under the authority of the hostile army. The occupation extends only to the territory where such authority has been established and can be exercised."[14] Article 43 of the Hague Regulations sets forth one of the primary legal duties of an occupying power. Because "[t]he authority of the legitimate power [has] in fact passed into the hands of the occupant," the occupant "shall take all the measures in his power to restore, and ensure, as far as possible, public order and safety, while respecting, unless absolutely prevented, the laws in force in the country."[15]

The text of article 43 of the Hague Regulations provides ample authority to the United States to change Iraqi law, including the fundamental change of Iraqi government institutions. Article 43 empowers an occupant to modify an occupied nation's laws if it is necessary to restore and ensure "public order and safety." Given the nature of the current Iraqi regime, the United States may need to make extensive changes to Iraqi laws, including a substantial overhaul of Iraqi government institutions, in order to ensure public order and safety.

Further, it is important to emphasize that even if the Hague Regulations were read to impose a stricter standard upon United States conduct, it would not legally bind our military occupation in Iraq. The Hague Regulations do not govern the U.S. conflict with Iraq because Iraq is not a party to Hague. Article 2 of Hague makes clear that its provisions apply only to armed conflicts between parties. Thus, the international law that applies to the United States is actually that created by custom and state practice, and to the extent that the text of article 43 and state practice deviate, the latter would control rather than the former. In any event, state practice would be relevant even if the Hague Regulations applied of their own force because it would illustrate how nations have interpreted article 43 over time.

In the period between the Hague Regulations and the signing of the Geneva Conventions of 1949, occupying nations often instituted changes in the laws and governmental institutions of the occupied territory. During World War I, for example, when Germany occupied Belgium, it supplanted the Belgian court system and divided Belgium into separate administrative regions. Germany also enacted new legislation governing trade, commerce, banking, and welfare, and raised taxes.[16] When Great Britain occupied French and Italian colonies in North Africa during World War II, it replaced the colonial governments with administrative divisions.[17] It also established new government systems, including a new judicial system, when the local administrative system in Somalia collapsed.[18] During the Allied occupation of Fascist Italy, the United States and Great Britain established an Allied Military Government of Occupied Territories that eliminated all Fascist institutions in Italy, removed Fascists from power, and repealed laws that discriminated on the basis of race, creed, or color. These developments were probably inevitable due to article 43's ambiguity. Nothing in the text of the phrase "unless absolutely prevented" establishes any substantive standard for what grounds must exist to overcome the presumption in favor of the status quo.[19] And in interpreting this vague text, occupying nations generally will have powerful motives for interpreting article 43 as broadly as possible. By the end of World War II, state practice had established the authority of an occupying power to implement fundamental changes in the laws and government of an occupied country.

The Fourth Geneva Convention

In response to Axis atrocities during World War II, an attempt was made in the Fourth Geneva Convention ("Geneva IV") to clarify the laws of occupation.[20] Geneva IV formally recognized the authority of an occupying nation to alter local laws. Un-

[14] Hague Convention, Annex, art. 42, 36 Stat. 2306.

[15] Hague Convention, Annex, art. 43, 36 Stat. 2306 (emphasis added).

[16] Eyal Benvenisti, The International Law of Occupation, 40, (1993).

[17] *See id.* at 73.

[18] *See id.* at 73–74.

[19] *See id.* at 13 ("[T]he meaning of 'unless absolutely prevented' remained conveniently vague. . . . The requirement to 'respect' the existing laws 'unless absolutely prevented' has no meaning of its own, since the occupant is almost never absolutely prevented, in the technical sense, from respecting them.").

[20] Convention (IV) Relative to the Protection of Civilian Persons in Time of War, Aug. 12, 1949, 6 U.S.T. 3516.

like the case with the Hague Regulations, both the United States and Iraq are parties to Geneva IV. The terms of the Convention apply to any military conflict between the two countries and to the U.S. occupation of Iraq.

Article 64 of Geneva IV gives the United States significant authority to alter the laws of Iraq during the occupation. Article 64 provides that " the penal laws of the occupied territory shall remain in force, with the exception that they may be repealed or suspended by the Occupying Power in cases where they constitute a threat to its security or an obstacle to the application of the present Convention."[21] Article 64 then states:

> [T]he Occupying Power may ... subject the population of the occupied territory to provisions which are essential to enable the Occupying Power to fulfill its obligations under the present Convention, to maintain the orderly government of the territory, and to ensure the security of the Occupying Power, of the members and property of the occupying forces or administration, and likewise of the establishments and lines of communication used by them.

The Red Cross commentary to Geneva IV states that article 64 of the Convention "expresses, in a more precise and detailed form, the terms of Article 43 of the Hague Regulations, which lays down that the Occupying Power is to respect the laws in force in the country "unless absolutely prevented."[22] Article 64, however, contains two important differences from Article 43. First, article 64 establishes a much weaker presumption in favor of the status quo, and it applies it only to the criminal laws. Second, article 64 does not limit to criminal laws the "provisions" to which the occupied territory may be subject. We may infer from this language that an occupying power may take measures under article 64 that include constitutional, civil, or administrative law as well as criminal.

Article 64 and customary international law empower the United States to impose "provisions" for a variety of enumerated purposes, without regard to whether such provisions can or cannot be reconciled with current law, and absent any strong presumption in favor of the status quo ante. For instance, article 64 explicitly empowers an occupant to institute those measures essential "to maintain[ing] the orderly government of the territory, and to ensur[ing] the security of the Occupying Power, of the members and property of the occupying forces or administration, and likewise of the establishments and lines of communication used by them."[23] In this respect, Geneva IV memorialized state practice under the Hague Regulations, which recognized an occupant's expansive authority to alter laws, including government institutions, in order to maintain the security of its military forces, preserve its military gains, and maintain domestic order. Occupying nations possess the authority to dismantle institutions that pose a threat to domestic or international peace and order, such as the Nazi regime in Germany. Commentators have also construed state practice to include all of the legitimate purposes of war, such as the promotion of democracy and the protection of fundamental human rights.[24]

The United States may reasonably conclude that institutions of the former Hussein regime pose a substantial threat to the security of the Armed Forces during the occupation of Iraq. Consequently, in order to protect the safety of the U.S. Armed Forces during an occupation of Iraq, it would almost certainly be necessary for Iraqi law to be changed so that these government institutions are dismantled. The preservation of the forms of the Hussein regime could also represent a danger to the national security of the United States. As Congress has found, the Iraqi government has generally demonstrated a continuing hostility to the United States. The Iraqi government has harbored and aided international terrorist organizations that threaten the lives and safety of American citizens. Just last year, Congress found that the current Iraqi regime posed a continuing threat to the national security of the United States, due to its possessions of chemical and biological weapons,

---

[21] Geneva Convention (IV) Relative to the Protection of Civilian Persons in Time of War, Aug. 12, 1949, 6 U.S.T. 3516, 3558.

[22] Jean S. Pictet, ed., *Commentary, IV Geneva Convention Relative to the Protection of Civilian Persons in Time of War,* 335, (1958) ("*Commentary on Fourth Geneva Convention*").

[23] 6 U.S.T. at 3558.

[24] *See e.g.*, Davis P. Goodman, *The Need for Fundamental Change in the Law of Belligerent Occupation,* 37 Stan. L. Rev. 1573, 1585-86 (1985) ("occupiers consider themselves absolutely prevented fromrespecting local law whenever it hinders the realization of the legitimate purpose of occupation"); *id.* at 1590 ("If the purpose of the conflict is to rid the occupied territory of a form of government objectionable to the belligerent occupier, the occupier will not respect the existing political structure while waiting for the final determination of the conflict.").

pursuit of nuclear weapons capability, and support for terrorist organizations.[25] Congress specifically noted Iraq's capability and willingness to use weapons of mass destruction and the risk that the current Iraqi regime would employ those weapons in an attack upon the United States or provide them to terrorists who would do so.[26] Iraq has also been a danger to the region. It has twice invaded its neighbors without provocation.

The historical record shows that the maintaining current Iraqi government institutions would constitute a threat to the national security of the United States and the safety of the U.S. Armed Forces in Iraq. Geneva IV and customary international law permit the United States to replace those institutions with others that would endanger neither the national security of the United States nor the safety of the U.S. Armed Forces. Given the Iraqi government's past behavior, the retention of the current Iraqi regime would be inimical to the establishment of peace and security in the Middle East.

Article 64 also expressly authorizes occupants to make alterations to laws of the indigenous government in order to protect rights guaranteed by Geneva IV. The rights afforded by Geneva IV sweep broadly. For example, article 27 provides that "[p]rotected persons are entitled, in all circumstances, to respect for their persons, their honour, their family rights, their religious convictions and practices, and their manners and customs." It establishes that "[t]hey shall at all times be humanely treated, and shall be protected especially against all acts of violence or threats thereof and against insults and public curiosity." It declares that "[w]omen shall be especially protected against any attack on their honour, in particular against rape, enforced prostitution, or any form of indecent assault." And it finds that "all protected persons shall be treated with the same consideration by the Party to the conflict in whose power they are, without any adverse distinction based, in particular, on race, religion or political opinion." All of these rights are subject to the qualification that "the Parties to the conflict may take such measures of control and security in regard to protected persons as may be necessary as a result of the war."[27]

Other provisions of Geneva IV require an occupying power to care for the population of an occupied country. Article 50 provides that "[t]he Occupying Power shall, with the cooperation of the national and local authorities, facilitate the proper working of all institutions devoted to the care and education of children." Under articles 55 and 56, the occupying power must, "[t]o the fullest extent of the means available to it," provide for "the food and medical supplies of the population," and "in particular, bring in the necessary foodstuffs, medical stores and other articles if the resources of the occupied territory are inadequate," as well as ensure and maintain, "with the cooperation of national and local authorities, the medical and hospital establishments and services, public health and hygiene in the occupied territory, with particular reference to the adoption and application of the prophylactic and preventive measures necessary to combat the spread of contagious diseases and epidemics."

Given the Iraqi government's abysmal record in the area of human rights, the United States cannot fulfill its obligations under Geneva IV without replacing the institutions of the Hussein regime. The regime maintained its hold on power only by brutally repressing the Iraqi people. It systematically murdered those perceived to be a threat to the regime. Hussein's security forces routinely tortured Iraqis, with beatings, rape, the breaking of limbs, and the denial of food, water, and medical treatment being commonplace. Needless to say, the regime did not tolerate political dissent, other political parties, or freedom of religion. It also displayed an utter disregard for the welfare of Iraqi women and children. Given the barbaric nature of the Hussein regime, the United States must eliminate the institutions of the Hus-

---

[25] Pub. L. No. 107–243, 116 Stat. 1498 (2002); *see also* Pub. L. No. 105–235, 112 Stat. 1538, 1540 (1998) (declaring that "Iraq's continuing weapons of mass destruction programs threaten vital United States interests and international peace and security").

[26] *See* Pub. L. No. 107–243, 116 Stat. 1498 (2002).

[27] An occupying power also must respect a number of rights provided to civilians charged with committing a criminal act during an occupation. Those prosecuted must be "promptly informed, in writing, in a language which they understand, of the particulars of the charges preferred against them, and shall be brought to trial as rapidly as possible." Art. 71, 6 U.S.T. at 3562. Additionally, those accused of crimes are guaranteed "the right to present evidence necessary to their defence and may, in particular, call witnesses." *Id.* Art. 72. Defendants also "have the right to be assisted by a qualified advocate or counsel of their own choice, who shall be able to visit them freely and shall enjoy the necessary facilities for preparing the defence." *Id.* Once convicted, protected persons continue to enjoy a range of rights under the Fourth Geneva Convention, including the right to "enjoy conditions of food and hygiene which will be sufficient to keep them in good health, and which will be at least equal to those obtaining in prisons in the occupied country," the right to "receive the medical attention required by their state of health," and "the right to receive any spiritual assistance which they may require." Art. 76, 6 U.S.T. at 3566.

sein government to carry out all of the duties placed upon it by Geneva IV and to protect the basic human rights given to the Iraqi people. Clearly, this will require the United States to establish a new Iraqi constitution and representative government institutions.

Although the drafters of Geneva IV formally recognized the expansive authority of an occupying nation to change the laws of an occupied nation, they did establish one significant substantive limitation. Article 47 forbids the introduction of any changes to the status quo that would deprive the population of Geneva IV rights. Article 47 states:

> Protected persons who are in occupied territory shall not be deprived, in any case or in any manner whatsoever, of the benefits of the present Convention by any change introduced, as the result of the occupation of a territory, into the institutions or government of the said territory, nor by any agreement concluded between the authorities of the occupied territories and the Occupying Power, nor by any annexation by the latter of the whole or part of the occupied territory.[28]

Therefore, the United States cannot alter the laws, including the government institutions of Iraq, in a manner that is inconsistent with the basic rights recognized by Geneva IV.

Some may argue that article 64 limits the occupying nation's authority to those changes that would last only during the occupation. While an occupying nation would possess the power to enact temporary measures necessary to fulfill its obligations under Geneva W, maintain order and security, and ensure its national security along with the security of its armed forces, article 64 and customary international law would not grant an occupying power the authority to make permanent changes in governmental institutions or constitutional law. To be sure, there will be circumstances in which an occupying power will need to suspend or modify the laws of an occupied nation only on a temporary basis. For example, in the midst of civil disorder, an occupant may resort to interim emergency measures, such as a curfew. In other situations, however, temporary measures will be plainly inadequate for an occupant to accomplish the legitimate purposes of occupation. In order for the United States to fulfill its obligations, maintain an orderly government, and protect its national security as well as the security of its armed forces while occupying Iraq, it almost certainly will be necessary for the United States to change Iraqi law to dismantle current Iraqi government institutions and create new ones to take their place.

CONCLUSION

International law provides the United States with ample authority to establish a new Iraqi constitution and democratic governmental institutions as part of its duty to secure public safety in Iraq, protect the basic human rights of Iraqis, and to restore international peace and security to the region.

Senator CORNYN. Thank you very much, Professor Yoo.

Professor Agawa.

STATEMENT OF NAOYUKI AGAWA, MINISTER AND DIRECTOR OF THE JAPAN INFORMATION AND CULTURE CENTER, EMBASSY OF JAPAN

Mr. AGAWA. Chairman Cornyn, Chairman Chafee, it is a distinct honor to testify before your subcommittee. I have submitted my written statement for the record, but I would like to briefly inform you of the making of the Japanese constitution in 1946, one instance in which the Americans were deeply involved in the making of somebody else's constitution, in the hope that that extraordinary story may assist you in thinking about how the United States wants to guide the constitution and the future of Iraq.

Please note that the views that I express today before your subcommittees are strictly my own, and do not in any way reflect the views of the Government of Japan, for which I currently work.

[28] 6 U.S.T. at 3548.

In order to grasp the time, place, and manner in which the new Japanese constitution was written, one needs to know the history surrounding that event in chronological order. Because my time is limited, I would just point out that the original draft of the 1946 constitution was prepared in English by a group of Americans without any Japanese participation, that the drafting was completed in a matter of a week in total secrecy in February 1946.

Professor Yoo just mentioned the fact that there are some legal bases for that kind of act, and I think that General MacArthur took care of that legal basis. Nevertheless, that's the fact.

The American occupation authority, known as GHQ, actually wanted to wait for the Japanese side to come up with a new constitutional draft, but for a variety of reasons decided to prepare the initial draft themselves, and handed it to the Japanese. The Japanese were certainly given opportunities to comment on and revise this GHQ draft after it was handed to them. Nevertheless, the American original has determined the character of the 1946 constitution to a large extent.

Well, having said that, I believe that the 1946 constitution has been largely successful. First and foremost, the 1946 constitution has functioned as the basic law of the land for the past 57 years. Its pacifist and democratic character, together with its emphasis on fundamental human rights, suited the mood of the Japanese people, who were tired of years of war and military control. Therefore, the 1946 constitution set the cornerstone for Japan's post-war democratization.

There are several specific examples of success.

Article 1 declared the Emperor to be the symbol of the State and of the unity of the people. It secured the Emperor's position constitutionally, while democratizing it by depriving him of all political powers, and by adding the new notion that his position is derived from the will of the people, with whom resides sovereign power. It ensured the gradual and peaceful democratization of Japan both during and after the occupation.

Article 9 proclaimed Japan's renunciation of war and its decision not to maintain armed forces, this helped to alleviate the fear of the resurgence of Japan's adventurous militarism.

Chapter III lists a variety of human rights, fundamental human rights. Many of these human rights provisions have functioned as a goal of the nation.

Chapters IV and V set forth provisions of the parliamentary system without substantial changes made to the 1890 constitution. This assured the continuity of government.

Chapter VI sets forth the provisions for the judiciary, that retained the basic structure of the pre-war judicial system, and that the Japanese judiciary continued to be base largely on the civil law tradition.

Article 96, last, sets forth a procedure for the revision of the 1946 constitution, and thus has given the Japanese people the option and freedom to change it in the future, although we have never changed the constitution so far.

Several aspects of the 1946 constitution have been less successful, however. First, some Japanese, because the initial draft was made by Americans, continue to believe that the 1946 constitution was imposed by the Americans on the Japanese people. Also, some believe that the Japanese Government's exceedingly restrictive interpretation of Article 9 has prevented Japan from becoming a full-fledged ally of the United States and from fully participating in international military action, that involvement of force necessary to maintain peace such as the first gulf war.

Some of the fundamental human rights provisions incorporated in Chapter III seem to reflect too many American legal ideas of the 1930's, *i.e.*, the bigger the government, the better. For example, the right to maintain the minimum standards of wholesome and cultured living, and the State's obligation to promote social welfare, security and public health in Article 25. These things have been difficult to enforce.

There are some other examples, but I am running out of time, so in conclusion, the American attempts to democratize Japan after World War II has been remarkably successful. The 1946 constitution was a major factor in that attempt. One must remember however, that the Japanese had experienced a healthy democracy in the 1920's, and that the post-war democracy was based on and grew from that experience.

As noted above, however, not every American-inspired measure worked successfully in post-war Japan, but no constitution is perfect, and it is now up to the Japanese people to fix it if and when necessary in accordance, again, with the freely expressed will of the people.

Thank you very much.

[The prepared statement of Mr. Agawa follows:]

Prepared Statement of Naoyuki Agawa

Introduction

Chairman Cornyn, and Chairman Chafee, and members of the subcommittees. It is a distinct honor to testify before your subcommittees on the making of the Japanese Constitution in 1946.

On August 15, 1945, Japan announced the acceptance of the Potsdam Declaration. That ended three and a half years of war between the United States and Japan. General MacArthur stepped onto Japanese soil 15 days later. Thus the occupation of Japan started and lasted approximately seven years. During that time, the United States together with other members of the Allied Powers undertook many measures to do away with the country's military control and revive Japan's democracy. Among them was the making of the new Japanese Constitution.

Almost 60 years later, the United States and its coalition partners are again finding themselves in charge of the occupation and democratization of Iraq. Among the tasks to be undertaken there in due course, I understand, is the making of the new Iraqi Constitution.

I would like to inform you of the making of the new Japanese Constitution in 1946 in the hope that that extraordinary story may assist you in thinking about how the United States wants to guide the constitutional future of Iraq. More specifically, I would like to give you examples of the American ideas incorporated into the Japanese Constitution, how they were incorporated, and which of these proved to be successful and which were not.

Please note that the views I express today before your subcommittees are strictly my own and do not in any way reflect the views of the government of Japan. I am testifying before your subcommittees strictly in the capacity of a constitutional scholar who has taught this subject at Keio University in Japan, the University of Virginia Law School and Georgetown University Law Center; therefore, I do not appear today sharing my views as a minister of the Embassy of Japan.

The History of the Making of the Japanese Constitution

In order to grasp the time, place and manner in which the new Japanese Constitution of 1946 (the "1946 Constitution") was written, it is perhaps useful briefly to narrate the history surrounding that event in chronological order.

Many believe that the writing of the 1946 Constitution started with the acceptance of the Potsdam Declaration, which presented the conditions for Japan's "unconditional surrender" to the Allied Powers. The Declaration, among other things, stated that "until there is convincing proof that Japan's war-making power is destroyed, [Japan] shall be occupied ..." Further, it stated that "the Japanese government shall remove all obstacles to the revival and strengthen[ing] of democratic tendencies among the Japanese people" and that "freedom of speech, of religion, and of thought, as well as respect for the fundamental human rights shall be established." Lastly, the declaration stated that "the occupying forces of the Allies shall be withdrawn from Japan as soon as these objectives have been accomplished and there has been established in accordance with the freely expressed will of the Japanese people a peacefully inclined and responsible government." Thus the Potsdam Declaration not only set Japan's surrender terms, but it also set the condition for the termination of the occupation, i.e., the demilitarization and democratization of Japan.

The General Headquarters of the Allied Powers (the "GHQ"), the occupation authority headed by General MacArthur, the Supreme Commander of the Allied Powers, did not initially embark on the making of a new Japanese Constitution. It was initially busy physically disarming the Japanese military establishment, arresting war criminals, freeing political prisoners and taking care of other such pressing matters. In fact, it was only in October 1945 that General MacArthur first suggested to then Prime Minister Kijuro Shidehara that the Japanese government consider necessary constitutional changes. Please note that the GHQ ruled Japan indirectly through the existing Japanese cabinet and the bureaucracy.

The Shidehara cabinet thereupon formed a committee to study the constitutional matters. This committee became known as the Matsumoto Committee, because it was headed by Dr. Matsumoto, a member of the cabinet who was also a noted legal scholar. The Matsumoto Committee was of the impression that (1) the GHQ was not in a particular hurry to make the constitutional changes and (2) the committee could deliberate the necessary constitutional changes free from the influence of the GHQ. Thus, The Matsumoto Committee began to study possible revisions to the existing Constitution promulgated in 1890 (the "1890 Constitution") in order to make it more democratic and accountable to the people without determining any concrete timetable for the actual revisions to take place.

This situation suddenly changed during the first week of February 1946. The Matsumoto Committee's drafts of the revised 1890 Constitution were leaked to and reported by a Japanese newspaper. General MacArthur's staff read these newspaper articles and found these proposed revisions to be inadequate for Japan's democratization. The principle of popular sovereignty, for instance, was not clearly set forth. Upon learning of these facts from his staff, General MacArthur asked the Government Section of the GHQ itself to start drafting a new Japanese Constitution. On February 3, the General gave the Government Section lawyers and others a one page note outlining a few of the most important principles to be included in the draft Constitution. This famous "MacArthur Note" included, among other things, a provision to retain the Emperor and another provision for the abolishment of war and armed forces, even for self-defense purposes. The Government Section secretly started its draft on February 4 and finished the task on February 10. This draft was approved by General MacArthur and officially became the GHQ Draft on February 12. The GHQ Draft was in English.

The GHQ Draft was shown to Dr. Matsumoto and a few other representatives of the Japanese government on February 13. Assuming that the American side intended to comment on the Committee's own draft Constitution that had been submitted to the GHQ a few days earlier, the Japanese delegation was stunned at the liberal tone of the GHQ Draft and declared that they were not ready to accept it. General Whitney, General MacArthur's deputy, stated in return that the acceptance of the GHQ Draft might be the only way for the Emperor to survive and for the current Japanese government to remain in control.

After several rounds of exchanges between the GHQ and the Japanese government, including a meeting between Prime Minister Shidehara and General MacArthur, the Japanese cabinet reluctantly agreed to prepare a new draft in Japanese, based on the GHQ Draft. This new round of drafting started on February 27 and was completed on March 2. The Japanese government lawyers submitted this new draft to the GHQ on March 4. The GHQ found this new draft was still inadequate. An all-night session to conform it to the GHQ Draft pursued, and this task was completed on March 5 with MacArthur's approval. On March 6, the Japanese cabinet approved this new draft and publicly released it as the Government Draft.

The Government Draft was submitted to the Diet and the Privy Council, the Emperor's advisory body, in accordance with the revision procedures of the 1890 Constitution as set forth therein. After lively debates and a fair number of revisions, the final Government Draft was adopted and proclaimed as the 1946 Constitution on November 3, 1946, effective May 3, 1947.

On September 8, 1951, Japan concluded a peace treaty in San Francisco with the United States and other Allied Powers. The peace treaty became effective on April 28, 1952 after its ratification by a majority of the signatories to the treaty. Thus Japan's occupation ended and the country regained its full independence.

Has the 1946 Constitution Been Successful?

I believe that the 1946 Constitution has been largely successful. This assessment is based on several factors.

First and foremost, despite initial opposition to some of the new ideas incorporated in the GHQ Draft and the Government Draft, the 1946 Constitution has functioned as the basic law of the land for the past 57 years. In fact, when the Government Draft was made public on March 6, 1946, the majority of the Japanese people favorably received it. Its pacifist and democratic character together with its emphasis on fundamental human rights suited the mood of the Japanese people who were tired of years of war and military control. It is fair to say, therefore, that the 1946 Constitution set the cornerstone for Japan's post-war democratization.

More specifically, Article I of the 1946 Constitution incorporated the revolutionary notion of the Emperor as the "symbol of the State and of the unity of the people." This provision has worked remarkably well. On the one hand, it secured the Emperor's position constitutionally, thus allowing the ancient tradition to survive the postwar turmoil. On the other hand, it democratized the Emperor by depriving him of all political powers and by adding the new notion that his position is derived from the "will of the people with whom resides sovereign power." Under the 1890 Constitution, in theory the Emperor retained all the rights of sovereign and reigned over and governed the Empire of Japan. Although the conservatives in Japan strongly resisted the idea of turning the Emperor into a mere figurehead, the Emperor as the spiritual symbol of the nation and not a political power actually conformed well to Japan's age-old political tradition and thus has functioned well. In my view, maintaining the Emperor tradition in Japan is MacArthur's greatest achievement in connection with the 1946 Constitution. It assured the peaceful and gradual democratization of Japan both during and after the occupation.

Article 9 of the 1946 Constitution incorporated another revolutionary notion of the renunciation of war. This provision also served its purposes particularly well for Japan's first 30 to 40 postwar years. In order to smoothly return to the international community, the Japan that was perceived in the 1930's as an aggressor in the Asia-Pacific region had to project the image of a born-again, peace-loving country. Article 9 proclaimed Japan's renunciation of war and its decision not to maintain armed forces. This helped to alleviate the fear of the resurgence of Japan's adventurous militarism, a feeling shared at the time by many countries and peoples surrounding Japan. It also made the Japanese sincerely aspire to become a truly peace-loving nation. The result is a Japan today that promotes peace worldwide largely through non-military means.

Also, importantly, Chapter III of the 1946 Constitution lists a variety of fundamental human rights. As a matter of concrete policy, the Japanese found some of them difficult to implement immediately because they were so idealistic and because the Japanese government had little resources to realize them. However, many of these "rights" provisions have functioned as the goals of the nation. The Japanese aspired to achieve these goals and to rebuild a country that is based upon and respects these fundamental human rights. For instance, Article 24 of the 1946 Constitution promulgated the equality of the sexes. Japanese women had not been treated as equals to men for historical and cultural reasons throughout most of Japanese history, and were inspired by this provision. Since then, they have significantly improved their social standing in Japan. It is perhaps fair to say that postwar Japan has respected people's "life, liberty and pursuit of happiness" and "equal[ity] under the law" to the greatest extent possible as provided in Articles 13 and 14 of the 1946 Constitution.

In addition, the 1946 Constitution maintained the parliamentary (the Diet) system without substantial changes made to the one under the 1890 Constitution. This assured the continuity of government. There were some important changes in this area, too. For instance, the 1946 Constitution specifically made the Cabinet directly responsible to the Diet, thus reviving and strengthening the 1920's democratic tradition that thrived in Japan before the military took control of the country. The 1890 Constitution had no express provision for the Cabinet's accountability to the Diet although by the 1920's it had become customary for the Cabinet to resign at the displeasure of the Diet. Also, the Prime Minister was given the authority to appoint and remove members of his cabinet. Nevertheless, the parliamentary system as a whole was not materially changed from the pre-war model. The drafters of the GHQ draft could have tried to institute a more American style of government by establishing clearer separations of power and creating a more independent executive branch of the government. However, these Americans knew and respected the Japanese' pre-war democratic experiences and traditions. Therefore, these drafters left the existing system intact. That worked well for Japan's needs.

Similarly, while the 1946 Constitution made the Japanese judiciary more independent and encouraged it to be more "rule of law" oriented in order to protect the fundamental human rights of the Japanese people, it respected and retained the basic structure of the pre-war judiciary system. Thus, the Japanese judiciary continued to be based largely upon the civil law tradition that was originally introduced from Germany and France. In fact, the person who worked on the reform of the Japanese judiciary system within the GHQ was Judge Opler, a naturalized American citizen who was a former judge in pre-Nazi Germany. He advised the GHQ not to introduce too much of the American judicial system, such as the election of judges. This suggestion has also worked well for Japan.

Lastly, the American drafters provided for the procedures for the revisions of the 1946 Constitution in Article 96. Some of the American drafters maintained that the provisions for fundamental human rights in Chapter III should be made non-amendable lest the Japanese people be deprived of these rights after the Americans left Japan. However, others argued and prevailed that the American drafters should not bind the future generations of the Japanese to what the Americans thought to be the most important constitutional principles. Thus, the Japanese have retained the freedom to amend the 1946 Constitution partly or in its entirety in accordance with the procedures set forth in Article 96. Interestingly, the 1946 Constitution has never been amended. Constitutional scholars have debated why the Japanese are so reluctant to amend the Constitution. Nevertheless, the insertion of the amendment procedures has given the Japanese people the option and freedom to change it in the future. It therefore weakens the argument that this Constitution was imposed on the Japanese by the Americans.

Certain Aspects of the 1946 Constitution That Are Less Successful

Several aspects of the 1946 Constitution have been less successful or totally unsuccessful.

First, some Japanese continue to believe that the 1946 Constitution was "imposed" by the Americans on the Japanese people and that it therefore lacks legitimacy. They still find offensive that the first draft of the 1946 Constitution was prepared in English by a group of Americans, and furthermore that it was done in an extremely short period of time and in complete secrecy. Those Japanese do not recall themselves "proclaim[ing] that sovereign power resides with the people" and "firmly establish[ing] this Constitution" as the Preamble to the 1946 Constitution states. Some believe that the 1946 Constitution is badly written as a matter of Japanese prose because the original draft was in English. In fact, a top secret directive from Washington to General MacArthur issued on January 7, 1946 entitled SWNCC 228 (the State-War Navy Coordinating Subcommittee for the Far East directive number 228) specifically stated that "[o]nly as a last resort should the Supreme Commander order the Japanese Government to effect the constitutional changes], as the knowledge that they had been imposed by the Allies would materially reduce the possibility of their acceptance and support by the Japanese people for the future." However, some Japanese had strong counter-arguments to this position. For instance, some scholars argue that because the Diet debated and amended the Government Draft in a relatively free fashion in the latter half of 1946, the Japanese people did have an opportunity to express their will in the making of the 1946 Constitution through their representatives. Scholars also argue that the Japanese have so far chosen not to amend the 1946 Constitution, indicating that the nation as a whole has approved of it and liked it. Also, the GHQ Draft was prepared in haste for several good reasons, for example, among other things, General MacArthur's wish to avoid Soviet Russia's intervention in his occupation policy, in order to prevent communist-led insurgency in Japan and to protect the Emperor from indictment as a war criminal. Nevertheless, because the first draft of the 1946 Constitution was prepared by a group of Americans without participation of any Japanese, I believe that this factor has harmed the legitimacy of the 1946 Constitution to a certain degree.

In addition, certain substantive ideas incorporated into the 1946 Constitution by the American drafters tended not to function well or became outdated after a while. The foremost of this example is in Article 9. General MacArthur was perhaps very keen on demilitarizing Japan and perhaps sincerely believed in a harmonious post-war international order. As a result, he was adamant that the Japanese people forever renounce war and do away with all armed forces. Given the impracticality of rebuilding its war potential at the time, the Japanese obliged. The American policy makers, including General MacArthur, quickly regretted inserting this provision in the 1946 Constitution and tried to persuade the Japanese to rearm when the Cold War heated up and the Korean War began. However, the Japanese refused to rearm, quickly citing Article 9 and pointing out that it was the United States that originally insisted on the insertion of this provision. The Japanese people have liked Article 9 and post-war Japan has become a pacifist country. This is all good and well. However, some believe that the Japanese government's exceedingly restrictive interpretation of Article 9 has prevented Japan from becoming a full-fledged ally of the United States and from fully participating in international military actions involving use of force necessary to maintain peace, such as the first Gulf War. In addition, the lack of any provision in the 1946 Constitution setting forth the war and emergency power of the government has hindered Japan from preparing for any war or other emergencies, such as terrorist attacks. Here lies a lesson, perhaps, that a radical, substantive constitutional provision may, in the long run, not work.

Similarly, some of the fundamental human rights provisions incorporated in Chapter 111 of the 1946 Constitution seem to reflect too many of American liberal ideas of the 193O's. It is a known fact that the three American drafters of Chapter III were liberally-oriented non-lawyers and that they were eager to add everything that the United States Constitution did not have. (For that matter, only one member of the American drafting team was Republican.) The ideas included by the drafters are: the freedom to choose residence and occupation, and to divest nationality (Article 22); academic freedom (Article 23); marriage based only on the mutual consent of both sexes and the essential equality of the sexes pertaining to marriage and family (Article 24); the right to maintain the minimum standards of wholesome and cultured living and the State's obligation to promote social welfare, security and public health (Article 25); the right to receive an equal education (Article 26); the right and obligation to work (Article 27); and the right of workers to collectively organize, bargain, and act (Article 28). While these provisions are all for good causes, some of them proved to be difficult to implement as a matter of concrete policy and have functioned more as desirable standards. Also, some have criticized these provisions as too strongly oriented towards rights, freedom and individualism (individual liberty). The dissenters believe that the American drafters failed to incorporate some of the more traditional Japanese values such as family, community, seniority, and the nation, therefore allowing the post-war Japanese generation to become more selfish and less public-minded.

Chapter VI of the 1946 Constitution, concerning the judiciary, is another area in which some of the American ideas did not work particularly well. While the 1946 Constitution strengthened the Japanese judiciary and made it more independent, the American drafters were concerned about the possibility of judicial tyranny because of their recent experiences with the "old horsemen" of the United States Supreme Court during the New Deal Era. Accordingly, in the 1946 Constitution the drafters added measures such as term limits for the judges (Article 80); the mandatory retirement ages for the judges of the Supreme Court as well as of lower courts (Articles 79 and 80); and even the performance review and recall of the Supreme Court judges by the people through ballots every ten years (Article 80). Also, the American drafters omitted the word "property" after "life and liberty" from Article 31 of the 1946 Constitution, setting forth the due process principle lest the property rights be abused by the Supreme Court as was the case in the United States in the late 19th and early 20th centuries. These provisions proved to be more or less irrelevant. For historical and other reasons, the Japanese judiciary never became as powerful as the American judiciary. No Japanese Supreme Court judge has ever been removed by the ballot because the average age of their appointment to the Supreme Court is 64, their mandatory retirement age is 70, and therefore no one remains on the bench at the next round of review ten years later. For that matter, the Japanese Supreme Court has exercised its judicial review power very sparingly. The American drafters incorporated the doctrine of *Marbury* v. *Madison* in Article 81 of the 1946 Constitution in the hope that the Supreme Court would function as a check against the Diet and the Cabinet nullifying the laws, orders and regulations it finds to be unconstitutional. The Japanese Supreme Court has, however, held the statutes unconstitutional only about five times in the past 55 years. It has a tendency to defer to the legislative will of the Diet, which is defined as the "highest organ of state power" in Article 41. This is not necessarily a bad result. Some scholars in the United States may envy the judicial restraint exhibited by the Japanese courts. It is simply that the Japanese judiciary did not behave as the American drafters hoped or feared. All in all, provisions for the judiciary in the 1946 Constitution have had mixed results. The provisions have created a more independent judiciary, but did not create as strong and influential a system as the United States judiciary.

Conclusion

In summary, the American attempt to democratize Japan after WWII has been remarkably successful. The 1946 Constitution was a major factor in that attempt. More than anything else, it set the benchmark against which the progress of the Japanese democratization was measured. Today, Japan is a thriving free market democracy where basic human rights are protected and the political system accountable to the people is functioning. The Potsdam Declaration's desire to see the establishment of a "peacefully inclined and responsible government" in accordance with the "freely expressed will of the Japanese people" has been fulfilled. The Japanese people owe a lot of this success to the American ideas, including those of the American drafters of the 1946 Constitution. One must also remember, however, that the Japanese had experienced a healthy democracy in the 1920's and that the post-war democracy was based on and grew from that experience.

As noted above, however, not every American-inspired measure worked successfully in post-war Japan. Certain provisions of the 1946 Constitution did not work as expected or became obsolete over time. Many of them were provisions that reflected American constitutional experiences that did not take root in the Japanese soil. Others were the currently popular substantive ideas that were bound to become obsolete over time. It was also unfortunate that the initial drafting of the 1946 Constitution did not allow for any Japanese participation and had to be completed in such a short time.

Nevertheless, the American-drafted 1946 Constitution sowed seeds of democracy in Japan, and the Japanese people have lived with (and some have put up with) this Constitution for more than half a century. No constitution is perfect, and it is now up to the Japanese people to fix it if and when necessary in accordance again with the freely expressed will of the people.

Chairman Cornyn, Chairman Chafee, and subcommittee members, thank you for your time. I appreciate the honor and privilege of being allowed to express my views today.

Senator CORNYN. Thank you very much, Professor; and now for a view of the German example. Dr. Kommers, thank you for joining us today. Please give us your opening statement.

STATEMENT OF DONALD KOMMERS, JOSEPH AND ROBBIE PROFESSOR OF POLITICAL SCIENCE AND PROFESSOR OF LAW, NOTRE DAME SCHOOL OF LAW

Dr. KOMMERS. Senator Cornyn, I also want to thank you for the subcommittee's invitation, but with your indulgence I may have to leave a little earlier since I have a plane to catch back to South Bend, Indiana at 7 this evening, and I know the rush hour gets pretty terrific around 5 in the afternoon.

My statement is very short, really less than 4 minutes. As I understand my task, it's not to lay out a blueprint for rebuilding constitutional government in Iraq, but rather to indicate what lessons we Americans might draw from the allied effort to restart constitutionalism in Germany after World War II.

My written statement lists many of the differences between occupied Germany in 1945 and occupied Iraq in 2003. The German experience may nevertheless be relevant in several respects. The German experience confirms, I think, much of what has already been said here today on this panel and on the previous panel and what Senator Feingold had to say earlier in his remarks.

In what respects? First, the German experience shows that reestablishing constitutional government can only begin when the occupying power is fully in control, and only when law and order is fully restored. Second, rebuilding democracy must be the first responsibility of the occupied country.

Third, a spirit of trust and cooperation must define the relationship between the occupiers and the occupied. In addition, the educated classes and a critical mass of democratically inclined citizens must be willing and able to cooperate with the occupation.

Finally, and perhaps the most important lesson of all, given the German experience, is that the restoration of democratic constitutionalism must be a bottom-up, rather than a top-down affair, and it must reflect indigenous values and traditions.

Consider how the process worked in Germany. Already, in late 1945, the military Governors authorized Germans to rebuild their local and state governments, in some cases in artificially created territorial units. They initially selected the prime ministers of those territorial units, the top German officials charged with this task of rebuilding, but thereafter, these officials acted on their own, save for certain functions related to internal security and foreign trade. These local units evolved, interestingly enough, into dynamic working governmental systems jealous of their power and autonomy, and pretty much based on the German tradition of statecraft.

By mid-1946, elected State Parliaments and Prime Ministers were functioning under written constitutions, at least in the four states within the American zone. Local representatives of political parties licensed by American military authorities drafted these constitutions, and they did so on their own. They didn't have all that much American or any other allied help at the time. Although requiring the approval of the allies, these constitutions, as suggested, were home-made products rooted in Germany's democratic tradition.

With this foundation in place, then, at both local and regional levels, the allies turned their attention to West Germany as a whole, almost 3 years Germany's military defeat. Of course, the establishment of a national government would probably have taken much longer had it not been for the American determination to bring Germany into the Atlantic alliance, given the cold war in the background.

At any rate, in mid-1948, 3 years after Germany's defeat, the military Governors commissioned the Prime Ministers of the 11 reorganized states to convene a national assembly to write a new constitution for Germany. They specified that the new constitution must establish a Federal form of government, protect the rights of the respective states, and provide for the protection of individual rights and freedoms, and within the framework of these broad principles, Germans were free—subject to allied approval—to draft a constitution of their own choosing.

The Prime Ministers moved at once. They appointed a committee of experts, constitutional experts and international experts, all Germans, to prepare a draft constitution for the consideration of a national assembly. Twenty-five persons, all Germans, accomplished this task in 14 days. No Americans were present during the writing of this draft constitution.

The initiative then shifted to the state legislatures. They elected a constitutional convention composed of 65 delegates. The Allies did not interfere in these elections. All 65 delegates were members of political parties represented in the state legislatures. These parties, each of which was licensed by the occupation authorities, represented the main segments of German public opinion opposed to the Nazi state. Forty-four of these political party delegates were members of their respective state legislatures.

Over the next 10 months the assembly, known as the Parliamentary Council, produced the Basic Law which, in the course of time, would become one of the world's great constitutions. The military Governors monitored the making of the Basic Law, but they did not participate in its proceedings.

On some issues, such as the status of Berlin and the preservation of internal security, allied demands did prevail, but these decisions were driven by the experience of the cold war, a condition which has no relevance to Iraq.

Conflicts arose between the convention and the military Governors, particularly over the taxing power of the national government, but this and other conflicts were resolved by compromise, and generally to the satisfaction of the Germans. In fact, the military governors made a number of concessions. For example, they originally insisted on the popular ratification of the constitution, but gave way to the German view that the state legislatures should perform this function. They, the military governors, also agreed to more centralization of Federal authority than they were originally prepared to accept.

I conclude. Germany's Basic Law became one of the great success stories of the occupation. The basis of the success seems clear. The German people were allowed to create institutions of their own choosing, and founded on their own political, social, and even religious traditions. I want to suggest at the end that the Germans would not have accepted the basic law had they believed it was imposed from above or from outside, and I believe that the Iraqis must believe that any new government or constitution is also one of their own making.

I would suggest, finally, that in reconstructing or recreating a constitutional government, the Iraqis might find some guidance in Germany's Constitution, better known as the Basic Law. Interestingly, Germany's Basic Law has come to replace the United States Constitution as the main model of constitutional governance around the world. It's just amazing to note how many countries out there, at least 50 or 60, have patterned their constitutions on the German Basic Law.

Let me say why I think this is the case. First, Germany's Basic Law speaks in the language of duties as well as rights. Second, it promotes solidarity as well as individualism. Third, it includes a system of political representation, combing proportional representation with a single-member district system, which most observers see as fairer and more effective than the first-past-the-post system in the United States. Finally, and importantly, it recognizes the public role of religion while ensuring its free exercise. Each of these features seems well suited to the future of constitutional government in Iraq.

[The prepared statement of Dr. Kommers follows:]

PREPARED STATEMENT OF DONALD P. KOMMERS

As I understand my task, it is not to lay out a blueprint for rebuilding constitutional government in Iraq, but rather to indicate what lessons Americans might draw from the Allied effort to restart constitutionalism in Germany after World War II. This committee should bear in mind, however, that Occupied Germany of 1945 is not the occupied Iraq of 2003. The two situations are entirely different, although the German experience may provide guidelines for political reconstruction in Iraq.

Allow me to list the main differences in the two situations: First, we invaded Iraq to remove its rulers and thereby to liberate its people; we invaded Germany to smash an enemy nation and to overpower its people. Second, Germany in 1945 was disgraced, disspirited, and dismembered; Iraq in 2003 survives with most of its infra-structure intact, its territory unified, and its people aroused. Third, the Germans mounted no armed opposition to the Occupation; Hussein loyalists, by contrast, are fighting back and killing Americans. Fourth, Iraq is pockmarked by tribalism, ethnic division, and religious radicalism, blotches on the polity conspicuous for their absence in occupied Germany. Finally, Germany's unconditional surrender validated the Allied Occupation, even in the eyes of most Germans, a legal reality far from clear in the case of Iraq's occupation.

Nevertheless, the German experience may be relevant to Iraq in these respects: First, reestablishing constitutional government can only begin when the occupying power is fully in control and only when law and order have been fully restored. Second, rebuilding democracy must be the first responsibility of the Iraquis. Third, a spirit of trust and cooperation must define the relationship between the occupiers and the occupied. Finally, the educated classes and a critical mass of democratically-inclined citizens must be willing and able to cooperate with the Occupation.

Perhaps the most important lesson of all is that the restoration of democratic constitutionalism must be a bottom-up rather than a top-down affair, and it must reflect indigenous values and traditions. (The top-down model worked in Japan because of that country's compliant political culture and the desire of its people to imitate American "know-how.") Top-down would not have worked in Germany, and is unlikely to work in Iraq.

Consider how the process worked in Germany. Already in late 1945, the Military Governors authorized Germans to rebuild their local and state governments. They selected the top German officials charged with this task, but thereafter these officials acted on their own save for certain functions related to internal security and trade relations beyond their respective zones of occupation. By mid-1946, elected parliaments and prime ministers were functioning under written constitutions, at least in the four states of the American Zone. Local representatives of political parties licensed by American military authorities drafted these constitutions. Although requiring the approval of the Allies, the constitutions were home-made products rooted in Germany's democratic tradition, and they were largely duplicates of the state constitutions in force during the Weimar Republic. Successful parliamentary democracies emerged from this bottom-up process of reconstruction.

With this foundation in place at both local and regional levels, the Allies turned their attention to the national level. (The reestablishment of the national government would probably have taken much longer had it not been for the American determination to incorporate West Germany into the Anti-Soviet Atlantic Alliance.) In mid-1948—three years after Germany's defeat—the Military Governors commissioned the prime ministers of the eleven reorganized states to convene a national assembly to write a new constitution for Germany. They specified that the new constitution must establish a federal form of government, protect the rights of the respective states, and provide for the protection of individual rights and freedoms. Within the framework of these broad principles, Germans were free, subject to Allied approval, to draft a constitution of their own making.

The prime ministers moved at once. They appointed a committee of experts to prepare a draft constitution for the assembly's consideration. Twenty-five persons—all Germans—accomplished this task in 14 days. No Americans were present during this period. The initiative then shifted to the state legislatures. They elected the assembly's 65 delegates. There was no Allied interference in these elections. All 65 delegates were members of political parties represented in the state legislatures. Fifty-four of the delegates—again all Germans—were members of these legislatures. Over the next ten months, the assembly—known as the Parliamentary Council—produced the Basic Law, which in time would become one of the world great constitutions. The Military Governors monitored the making of the Basic Law, but they did not participate in its proceedings.

Conflicts arose between the convention and the Military Governors, particularly over the taxing power of the national government. But this and other conflicts were resolved by compromise and generally to the satisfaction of the Germans. In fact, the Military Governors made a number of concessions. For example, they originally insisted on the popular ratification of the Constitution, but gave way to the German view that the state legislatures should perform this function. They—the Military Governors—also agreed to more centralization of federal authority than they were originally prepared to accept.

Germany's Basic Law became one of the great success stories of the Allied Occupation. The basis of the success seems clear: The German people were allowed to create institutions of their own choosing and founded on their own political, social, and even religious traditions. Yet the Basic Law marked out a new beginning by its codification and promotion of a constitutional morality that rejected the political pathologies of the past. The Occupation experience shows that in the right set of circumstances, which may or may not exist in Iraq, military authorities can transform a once-outlaw nation into a promising constitutional democracy.

Senator CORNYN. Thank you very much, Dr. Kommers.

Professor Howard, I welcome you to this panel and I mentioned when, I believe, you were out of the room that we first met, and I have to say that you are at least in part a reason why I am interested in this subject, during my time at the University of Virginia and my participation in the master's of law program at the University of Virginia Law School and the thesis that I ended up writing on the creation of the Texas constitution of 1845, but enough of that.

We'd be pleased to hear your opening statement.

STATEMENT OF A.E. DICK HOWARD, WHITE BURKETT MILLER PROFESSOR OF LAW AND PUBLIC AFFAIRS, UNIVERSITY OF VIRGINIA LAW SCHOOL

Mr. HOWARD. Mr. Chairman, we will agree that the Texas constitution of 1845 was one of the great constitutional documents of all time.

May the record show that.

Mr. Chairman, thank you for inviting me. I suspect that my chief credentials for being here are that I teach constitutional law at the University of Virginia. Our founder was Thomas Jefferson, our first rector was James Madison. As constitutional credentials go, those aren't bad, I suppose.

I cut my teeth, in constitutional terms, in working on the present Virginia constitution. In more recent years, I've had the privilege of sitting at the elbows of drafters of constitutions in a number of other countries, especially post-Communist countries in Central and Eastern Europe. This has sparked in me an interest in comparative constitutionalism and, in particular, the question of how constitutional ideas travel, how they get from one place to another, what takes, what doesn't take, whether there are universals which drafters ought to be concerned with, or ultimately whether constitutions are a product of culture, tradition, history, and circumstance.

A subset of that question for an American audience and, I think, for all of us is whether there is some instructive value in the American experience, though it may now be nudged aside, my colleague insists, by the German experience.

I have submitted a written paper, so I will only summarize the points I made there. I undertake in that paper a case study of post-Communist, post-1989 Central and Eastern Europe. There one finds an interesting eclecticism where the drafters in those countries drew where they could on their own experience, which was often very mixed and checkered and broken, then drew to some extent on Western Europe's experience, to no one's surprise, since they felt themselves rejoining the family of Europe.

They didn't, at least in obvious terms, draw on the American experience. They were much closer to Western Europe. They drew as well on international documents, very much part of the world since World War II. These offer another source for drafters—U.N. covenants, OSCE documents like the Helsinki and Copenhagen documents, and others.

I won't take the time here to rehearse the history of how American ideas have, in fact, influenced other places. Again, I have it in my paper. There have been a number of historical chapters—France in the revolutionary period, liberal Europe in 1848, the Philippines as our colony after 1900, the Wilsonian period after World War I (making the world safe for democracy, as Wilson put it), Japan and Germany after World War II (two quite important and very instructive stories for our purposes), and then, finally, the successive waves of democracy, the Mediterranean in the 1970's (Spain's 1978 constitution is an important point of reference), the South American countries in the 1980's, Central and Eastern Europe after 1989, and, of course, South Africa at about the same time.

It's interesting to hear people debate the relevance, if any, for other countries of the American constitutional experience. Some of my scholarly colleagues argue that it really has no place in the drafting of other constitutions. For one thing, an 18th century document doesn't look like much of a model for people drafting constitutions in the 21st century. Moreover, some scholars would argue that the American experience has been so exceptional, so unlike the rest of the world, that the conditions that gave rise to constitutionalism here simply cannot be replicated elsewhere.

I understand those arguments. But I think they miss the point that the value of the American experience lies not in taking the actual document as a template and trying to copy something out of it, but rather in plumbing it to its depths for the underlying core values that it represents—values such as federalism. Around the world, federalism has been put to service in a number of ways. It doesn't have to be American-style formal constitutional federalism, but it can be other kinds of devolutionary arrangements. In addition to federalism, separation of powers, checks and balances, judicial review—all of these are principles in which the American experience has been very important, though they don't exhaust their various possibilities.

I think, finally, I would suggest that one would like to test the prospects for constitutional democracy, in Iraq or in any other place, by several observations. I would like to define the search, not simply being for our Constitution, but being a search for constitutional liberal democracy. By this I mean democracy accountable to the people, liberalism, i.e., the protection of the individual, and constitutionalism, enforcing the Constitution.

In my paper, I've suggested several factors that might be held up as ways of thinking about whether a constitutional enterprise may be successful or not. These include protection from foreign aggression, economic prosperity, a constitutional culture, an open society, the existence of a civil society, and a State based finally on civic and not ethnic or national principles. I think most of those concepts are fairly well-known.

Ultimately I agree with what I've heard at both panels this morning, that the Iraqi people must themselves do the job. They must understand that they are the proprietors of the new constitution. But I think they are well-informed if they take stock of what has happened in other countries like Japan and Germany, what's happened here in America, what the teachings of the modern constitutional period are.

Mr. Chairman, thank you.

[The prepared statement of Mr. Howard follows:]

PREPARED STATEMENT OF A. E. DICK HOWARD

In recent years I have had the privilege of sitting at the elbows of constitution-makers in countries seeking to lay the foundations of constitutional liberal democracies in those countries. Some years earlier, I cut my teeth in the art of constitution-making when I was involved in the drafting of Virginia's present state constitution. I have also consulted with other states seeking to revise their constitutions. But no experience has been so instructive as watching constitutions take shape in the context of other lands and cultures.

This experience in comparative constitutionalism has drawn me to ask questions about the extent to which one country can assist in, or make judgments about, another country's constitutional journey. How well do constitutional ideas travel, especially across the boundaries of different cultures or legal systems? Are there universal values by which the relative success of a constitutional system may be measured? Or, as some people argue, must constitutions ultimately be grounded in a country's culture, history, traditions, and circumstances? For Americans, there is the specific question: what relevance does the American constitutional experience have for other countries?

THE EXPERIENCE OF CENTRAL AND EASTERN EUROPE

To sharpen these questions, consider the experience of the countries of Central and Eastern Europe. After the collapse of communism, each of those countries set out to write new constitutions and to design institutions thought to promote constitutional liberal democracy. Drafters in those countries (Poland, Hungary, etc.) had several sources on which they could draw in devising new constitutions.

1. In some cases they could look back to their own indigenous sources and experience. For example, Poles recall the traditions of constitutionalism associated with the memorable Constitution of May 3, 1791. Hungarians have a strong tradition of the rule of law, having its roots as early as the Golden Bull of 1222. But such traditions are often fragmentary and remote, Few countries in Central and Eastern had any extended experience with either constitutionalism, democracy, or the rule of law before 1989 (Czechoslovakia's vibrant democracy between the world wars was a notable exception).
2. Countries in Central and Eastern Europe have been able to look—and have looked—to the experience of Western Europe. Western Europe is, of course, the seat of much of the core of modern constitutional democracy (such as the teachings of the Enlightenment), but also the sources of many of our basic constitutional principles (such as the separation of powers). Moreover, constitutionalism, democracy, and the rule of law have taken hold in manifest ways in Western Europe since World War II. Germany, rising from the ashes of World War II, has become a admirable example of constitutional democracy. Spain, moving beyond the legacy of Franco, has become in every respect a modern European state. With these and other examples to study, drafters

in Central and Eastern Europe have fashioned constitutional systems which in many obvious ways are modeled upon Western Europe. For example, Germany's Constitutional Court has proved the inspiration for the creation of constitutional courts throughout Central and Eastern Europe.

3. International norms and documents are an important source for constitution-makers in post-communist Europe, just as they are in other parts of the world. Especially is this true in giving shape and protection to human rights. Thus drafters look to such international documents as United Nations conventions and to regional arrangements such as the European Convention on Human Rights and OSCE's Helsinki and Copenhagen documents. Also, it is common for post-communist constitutions to state that international law and agreements shall be domestic law within a country.
4. One would suppose that constitution-makers in Central and Eastern Europe would study the experience of their neighbors in the region. Especially might this seem helpful when these countries have shared many of the problems of the post-communist world, such as the destruction of civil society during the communist era, the stultifying effects of command economies, and the cynicism about public life which was spawned by those years. It is my impression, however, that drafters in the region have not cared much to study their nearest neighbors' experience. This may partly be a consequence of historic enmities in the region. But it may also underscore the powerful pull of western models, especially in light of the pervasive wish of countries in Central and Eastern Europe to "rejoin" the family of Europe, in particular, to become members of the European Union.
5. Has the post-communist world looked to the American experience and to American ideas and models? A superficial look at new constitutions in the region might suggest that American influence has been slight. Throughout Central and Eastern Europe, one sees, for example, parliamentary systems rather than an American-style congressional system, presidential systems which look more to Western Europe (such as France) rather than to the United States, and constitutional courts resembling that of Germany rather than an American-style Supreme Court. The question of American influence—whether in post-communist Europe or in other countries (such as Iraq)—requires, however, a deeper enquiry than this superficial survey might suggest.

THE INFLUENCE OF AMERICAN CONSTITUTIONALISM: AN HISTORICAL PERSPECTIVE

The American revolutionary period was a time of remarkable innovation and accomplishment. Aware of their special place in history, the founders shaped such ideas as federalism, separation of powers, judicial review, and other concepts which have proved to be among the core principles of modern constitutionalism. not only in the United States, but in many other countries as well. American society differed in important ways from that of Europe; there was, for example, no monarchy and no legally entrenched social order. Even so, Europeans followed with fascination the evolution of American constitutionalism from the revolution, through the making of the Constitution, and beyond.

For two centuries and more, there has been intense traffic in constitutional ideas between America and other lands. Highlights of those exchanges include the following.

The Founding Era in France and America

The French Revolution, in 1789, brought close French attention to American ideas. Benjamin Franklin, immensely popular in Paris, undertook to spread news of what was happening in America, as did his successor, Thomas Jefferson. The Virginia Declaration of Rights (1776) influenced the drafting of France's Declaration of Rights of Man and the Citizen (1789). When the French National Assembly debated France's first constitution, moderate and radical factions invoked examples drawn from the experience with American state constitutions, especially Massachusetts and Pennsylvania. Ultimately, French constitutional development took a markedly different course from that of America, but it is instructive that in many ways it was America's founding documents that helped frame the debates in France.

Liberalism in the Nineteenth Century

In the early decades of the nineteenth century, liberal reformers in Europe and in South America invoked the United States as proof that liberal democracy could survive and flourish. When the revolutions of 1848 broke out in Europe, conventions meeting in France and Germany frequently dissected American institutions in deciding what a liberal constitution might look like in Europe. By this time,

Toqueville's *Democracy in America* had heightened interest in the American experience, especially federalism and judicial review. Germany's Paulskirche Constitution, drafted in Frankfort, was not in fact implemented, but its principles, building in part on American ideas (e.g., federalism and constitutional review), have reappeared in Germany's Basic Law of 1949. In South America, the age of Bolivar brought constitutions which were often modeled heavily on the United States Constitution. South American soil was, however, not yet fertile for such transplants, and these experiments were largely failures.

Political Evangelism in the Early Twentieth Century

When the United States acquired the Philippines as a result of the Spanish-American War, President McKinley described American policy as "benevolent assimilation." These plans included gradual development of self-government, the creation of a system of public education, and the transfer of American legal ideas. The Constitution adopted in 1935 owed much to American influence but drew upon other traditions as well. In 1946 the Philippines became independent.

The most famous effort to export American ideas in the early twentieth century was, of course, President Woodrow Wilson's aim, with the allied victory in World War I, to "make the world safe for democracy." Wilson did not think that other countries had to adopt an American-style constitution. But he did emphasize self-determination, free elections, the rule of law, individual rights, and an independent judiciary. The most successful democracy to rise from the ashes of World War I was Czechoslovakia, whose leading founder, Thomas Masaryk, had spent part of the war in the United States, working hard to influence American policy.

Japan and Germany After World War II

After the Japanese surrender in 1945, General Douglas MacArthur moved promptly to secure the drafting of a new constitution. Concerned that the Japanese elite, left to their own devices, would make little substantial change from the status quo, MacArthur instructed his military government to draft a constitution, which they did in a matter of days. Debate still continues, especially among Japanese politicians and scholars, over the extent to which the Constitution of Japan was imposed or has become in fact Japanese.

By the time drafting got underway on what became Germany's Basic Law of 1949, the Cold War was beginning to dominate American foreign policy. The occupying allied powers had a say, of course, in shaping German post-war policy. But, with the Americans and their allies seeing the Soviet Union as the greater threat, the Germans had a freer hand in the Basic Law's drafting. There are important ways in which the Basic Law has principles familiar to Americans, such as federalism and judicial review,. But the 1949 document owes much to Germany's own constitutional tradition, including the Paulskirche Constitution of 1949.

Waves of Democratization in the Latter Decades of the Twentieth Century

The spread of constitutionalism, democracy, and the rule of law came in waves in the closing decades of the twentieth century. The 1970s saw autocratic governments yield to democracy in Mediterranean countries—Greece, Portugal, and Spain. Spain's 1978 Constitution is especially important as a model for other post-authoritarian countries. Attention shifted to South America in the 1980s, notably to Argentina and Chile. The great year was 1989—the year the Berlin Wall came down and communism collapsed all over Central and Eastern Europe. The shock waves also hit South Africa, where the apartheid regime fell, and a new constitution came into effect in 1997.

American assistance to constitution-making and democratization in such places as post-communist countries has been undertaken both by public and private bodies. Typically the aid has taken the form of technical assistance, such as helping parliaments to update their processes, nurturing an independent judiciary, and assisting in the drafting of new constitutions and laws. An especially effective program is the American Bar Association's Central and Eastern European Law Initiative (now the Central European and Eurasian Law Initiative), which has sent hundreds of experts to work in scores of countries. Often the efforts of American advisors has been paralleled by advice and assistance from European governments and bodies, such as the Council of Europe's Venice Commission.

THE PLACE AND RELEVANCE OF THE AMERICAN CONSTITUTIONAL EXPERIENCE

When other countries write constitutions and set out to shape a constitutional regime, of what relevance is the American constitutional experience? What follows are arguments which lead some to conclude that the American experience is of limited value in other countries and cultures.

1. Constitutionalism must be understood as an expression of culture. Few would argue with this proposal if it is advanced as a caveat, namely, that one should always take culture into account in thinking about constitutions and constitutionalism. But some observers take the argument further, contending that there are no "universal" elements of constitutionalism. For example, by this view, community or group rights could be valued above individual rights.
2. American constitutionalism was the result of Enlightenment assumptions, steeped in British constitutionalism, and shaped in the historical settings of America. Some argue, therefore, that the teachings of American constitutionalism cannot be exported to other cultures. Such arguments often cite the failure of Latin American constitutions based on the US model and more recent problems in places such as the Philippines.
3. Even those who think the American experience is relevant and useful find limits in the United States Constitution as a model for foreign drafters. The document was written in the eighteenth century, reflects the insights of that era, and has required formal amendment (notably the post-Civil War amendments) and extensive judicial interpretation and gloss. Much of the American jurisprudence of rights results from judicial gloss rather than from the explicit constitutional text (for example, the process of "incorporation" doctrine by which guarantees of the Bill of Rights are applied to the states). Also, the United States Constitution is, in a sense, an incomplete document, in the sense that its framers assumed the existence and function of the states and therefore of state constitutions (documents which in many ways are rather more like constitutions in other countries).

All of these observations have force and ought to be taken into account, especially before assuming that what has worked well in America must surely work for other peoples as well. But the problems of comparative constitutionalism ought not to be turned into categorical barriers. The usefulness of the American experience does not lie in the formal text of the United States Constitution. It is to be found in the general principles which are reflected in American constitutionalism and, further, in the practical experience of making constitutional democracy work.

Many of the most basic ideas in American constitutionalism reflect norms that furnish at least presumptive value elsewhere. Examples include the following:

1. *Federalism.* Formal federalism, as charted by the Constitution, may or may not be appropriate in other countries. Federalism, however, is a system which has many variants and is found in one form or another around the world. Federalism and its cousins (such as devolution) is associated with values of pluralism, diversity, and local choices about local problems. Such arrangements may be especially important to defuse conflicts of nationality or ethnicity.
2. *Separation of powers.* This principle, celebrated by Montesquieu and refined by Madison, is a way of achieving limited government—one of the ultimate guarantees of individual rights. In its historical uses, it has been used to counter the tendency of such doctrines as popular sovereignty and legislative supremacy to become arbitrary or tyrannical.
3. *Judicial review.* Various devices have been used in an effort to keep a constitution's promises. These include popular will, separation of powers, and legislation. In the modern world, however, constitutions increasingly look to judicial review as a key means to enforce constitutional norms. John Marshall's insights in *Marbury* v. *Madison* have become a familiar part of constitutionalism around the world. One may well suggest that no American contribution to constitutionalism has been more pervasive or important than this one.

These ideas and principles are complemented by the practical experience of making American democracy work. Many countries have entered the age of constitutional democracy with little or no experience with such concepts as constitutionalism, democracy, and the rule of law. For example, for a half century the countries within the sphere of Soviet domination lived in a domain cut off from any such concepts. Thus American or other advisors can bring the fruits of hands-on experience in organizing political parties, conducting free and fair elections, nurturing a free and responsible press, creating an independent judiciary, and instilling the values of citizenship through civic education.

FACTORS BEARING ON THE PROSPECTS FOR CONSTITUTIONAL LIBERAL DEMOCRACY

It is not enough that a society be democratic. It must also be liberal and constitutional. Democracy seeks to assure that government is based upon the consent of the governed and is accountable to the people. But democracies should also be liberal, that is, committed to individual rights and freedoms, to the Lockean principle that the state depends on the individual, not the other way around. And democracies must also be constitutional, that is, there must be means to assure the enforcement of constitutional norms, even when that means negating a majoritarian judgment.

What are some of the factors bearing upon the prospects for the success of constitutional liberal democracy? Each person might draw up his or her own list, and one might debate the relative place and weight of each factor. But a list of factors would likely include at least the following. Note that the list goes well beyond those factors which can be incorporated into the text of a constitution.

1. A country should have sufficient military strength, as well as social and economic stability, to counter foreign aggression and to guard against internal subversion or unrest. Strength need not come, of course, solely from the country's own resources. A country may properly look to its allies, as, during the Cold War, so many democracies (not just weak ones) counted on American support in the event of Soviet aggression.
2. A vibrant constitutional culture often goes hand in hand with a healthy economy. I do not contend that, because countries are rich, they will necessarily be constitutional democracies. There are countries rich in oil, for example, which one would be slow to characterize as constitutional, liberal, or democratic. But it does seem fair to say that poor economic conditions often work to undermine any hope for constitutional democracy.
3. There should be a political culture—I would call it a constitutional culture—which encourages the values of constitutionalism, liberalism, democracy, and the rule of law. This implies a high level of literacy. But it also implies circumstances in which citizens have practiced the norms of cooperation, toleration, and forbearance associated with the fluctuating fortunes of causes, candidates, and parties. It means that those who lose an election turn the reigns of power over to the winners. It means that those who find that a victory in the legislative process is overturned on constitutional grounds by a court accept the principle of constitutional limits on government.
4. An open society, including free and responsible press and media, is the handmaiden of constitutionalism and democracy. There should be the means for open and effective communication both among the people and between them and their government.
5. Civil society should flourish. Private organizations—political parties, trade unions, interest groups, clubs, etc.—create an important buffer between the individual and the state. Such organizations offer a place of refuge for those who think that the politics of the moment are not in their favor. They offer training grounds for the qualities which make for effective citizenship and make possible the kind of collective voice and action which precludes the state's monopoly of power.
6. States should be based on the civic, rather than ethnic or national, principle. That is, all citizens should have equal standing in the society. There should not be "insiders" and "outsiders." If the state is not largely homogeneous in terms of religion, language, ethnicity, or culture, then there needs to be a widely felt commitment to toleration. To make constitutional liberal democracy work, the people must have a level of mutual trust, and ability to cooperate, rather than fragmenting into camps of hate and hostility.

Ultimately, history, culture, and circumstance will tell us much about the prospects for constitutionalism, democracy, and the rule of law in any country. Those who hope to see these values prosper in Iraq must understand Iraq itself—its people, its history, its culture, Some factors characterize the region, for example, the argument over the extent to which Islam is, or is not, ultimately compatible with constitutional liberal democracy. Other factors flow from Iraq's own history, for example, the question whether the parliamentary experience of he Hashemite years before 1958 has any useful legacy, or whether the middle class has been sturdy enough to survive the years of Saddani's repressions. Experts on Iraq will help inform these judgments. But those who would shape events in Iraq should also consult the lessons to be learned from transitions from totalitarian or authoritarian regimes elsewhere. The road to constitutionalism, democracy, and the rule of law takes one through many lands.

Senator CORNYN. Thank you, Professor Howard.
Mr. Kritz.

STATEMENT OF NEIL KRITZ, DIRECTOR, RULE OF LAW PROGRAM, U.S. INSTITUTE OF PEACE; ACCOMPANIED BY LOUIS AUCOIN

Mr. KRITZ. Thank you, Mr. Chairman. Thank you for the invitation. I am also obliged to note that the comments that I will give are my own, and don't represent the views of the U.S. Government or the U.S. Institute of Peace.

There are three vital and interrelated issues that are essential to establishment of the rule of law in Iraq, one being the constitution-making process that we're focused on primarily today, a second being the question of transitional justice, of how Iraqi society is going to deal with questions of accountability and the legacy of the crimes of the past regime, and the third being the broader challenge of legal reform within Iraq.

Each of these have the potential of being transformational for Iraqi society in very fundamental ways. They each share in common as well the fact that they need to be started immediately, but with the recognition that they are not short-term processes, and adequate time needs to be allocated to allow them to move forward properly.

Rushing or short-circuiting any of these exercises will be done only to the detriment of the ultimate result. That relates to the length of time that we need to remain committed to the process, the overall costs, and the period of time that we maintain boots on the ground in post-conflict societies like Iraq.

I would point as an example to our recent experience in Bosnia, where 7 years after the Dayton Accords former British MP Paddy Ashdown entered as High Representative in charge of moving the process forward. His first comment was that the international community finally had to get serious about the rule of law in Bosnia, or else the Dayton process could collapse like a house of cards. We still have troops on the ground more than 8 years later, in part because we have not paid enough attention to these fundamental processes we're discussing here today, and so I commend your attention to this issue.

My comments with respect to the constitution-making process emerge primarily from a 2-year study that the U.S. Institute of Peace has undertaken on post-conflict constitution-making processes. Through case studies of some 17 countries over the last 25 years, the study has attempted to examine the ways that the constitution-making process can be a means to advance national reconciliation and the building of peace, or alternatively may become an obstacle to not moving forward properly.

I'm accompanied here today by Professor Louis Aucoin of the Institute staff, who has been coordinating the project at the Institute.

Major powerholders and elite factions are inevitably going to play a major role in many post-conflict constitution-making process. Part of the challenge is to constrain their ability to monopolize that process. The final document should be more than simply a deal cut to divide the spoils between powerful factions on the ground today.

There are two tools that I would point to in particular in that regard. One is the notion of allowing adequate time for the process. A rapid rough-shod process is going to be nothing more than that simple deal between those who currently hold all the power. A more extended and open process that allows a variety of other factions to evolve and participate can facilitate lively challenge and debate within this exercise and be one important way of constraining the power of the few.

Another will be the adoption at the outset of the constitutional process of a set of basic rules that will govern both the process as well as at least the broad outlines of the substance of the ultimate document. This would be the place to initially enshrine basic recognition of principles of tolerance, pluralism, gender equality, religious and ethnic equality, possibly certain limitations on the future role of the military, and other basics, without predetermining the constitutional document.

If done properly, this process can be a potent tool for the empowerment and enfranchisement of a broader base within society, allowing a diverse variety of groups within civil society to emerge and to develop their own capacity to play a role in the debate on the future of Iraqi society. It would result in a diffusion of power from the few to the many. It can provide, as well, an important forum for various groups, particularly aggrieved groups within society, to articulate their visions and their concerns about the future distribution of power.

It would provide opportunities through a basic framework that creates a political space. One option in this regard is the use of an interim constitution. I'm reminded always of sitting in the South African constituent assembly, where an interim constitutional arrangement provided the political space to allow everyone from the Freedom Front on the far right to the Pan-African Congress on the far left to sit and debate the emergency powers under the new constitution in ways that they all told me afterwards would not have been possible without this kind of an interim process, which we're seeing emerge in an increasing number of cases.

A constitutional commission would be established that would have three basic functions. First, public education. This provides an important opportunity to educate the public on these broad principles noted earlier that should govern society in the future.

Second, and in a subsequent phase, a process of consultation of the public on specific questions that need to be addressed in the context of the constitution. This can provide various groups in society with a sense of ownership and can contribute to subsequent sustainability of the final product, as well as the potential for pressure on the part of those owners if and when those who subsequently hold power fail to implement and uphold the constitution.

From Rwanda to Albania, we've seen this process taking hold in important ways—in ways that, I would note, in some cases have transformed even the members of the constitutional commissions as they engage the public. They've changed their own opinions and transformed from representatives of their own factions to a more cohesive unit, looking at what makes sense for the future of the country.

Last, I would point to the role of the international community in this process. I would simply reiterate what has been said before. There is an appropriate role for the international community, including the United States, to play, but that's to provide neutral resources with respect to experiences in other countries with respect to basic constitutional principles without favoring any particular faction and without, as we've seen in some instances, having international experts serve as hired guns for one faction or another, enhancing only their capacity.

This can be formalized. In the case of Eritrea, the constitutional commission process included an international advisory committee of experts that helped to inform the process. It will be important that this include not only the U.S., but also those from other countries, because there is a rich body of experience that has emerged from many of them in recent years, and it will be important for Iraqis to be able to take advantage of that as well.

With that, thank you.

[The prepared statement of Mr. Kritz follows:]

PREPARED STATEMENT OF NEIL J. KRITZ

Introduction

In countries such as Iraq, a successful outcome requires a focus not only on the final document which emerges, but on the path to producing and adopting it. Indeed, the constitution-making process can be a transformational one for societies, if properly organized and given adequate attention and resources. These are among the lessons that emerge from an ongoing study that has been conducted over the past two years by the United States Institute of Peace on "Constitution-Making, Peace Building, and National Reconciliation," Through an examination of seventeen case studies of constitution-making processes around the world which have occurred over the course of the last twenty five years, focusing primarily on post-conflict transitions, the study is attempting to assess the constitution-making process for its potential for conflict resolution and prevention and for the maintenance of stable peace. To date, this review by a wide range of experts strongly suggest a basic message: perhaps more so than at any previous time in history, the process by which constitutions are made matters.

Interim Arrangements

The constitutional process is often facilitated by the establishment of interim arrangements. While this has taken a variety of forms, the essential characteristics are the following: (1) the clarification of basic legal rules and governmental structures during the interim period, allowing society to move forward with a minimum of disorder; (2) an interim framework that embodies sufficient changes from the prior system to clearly demarcate a break from the past and to immediately remove those elements that are clearly objectionable or repressive. The result can be an interim constitutional framework that opens adequate political space to enable all parties to participate and debate even hotly contentious constitutional issues in an atmosphere that guarantees their rights and interests pending the development of a final constitution.

Most of the cases included in the USIP study have involved some type of interim arrangement which has provided for some degree of stability during the period of the constitution-making process. In some cases, (Rwanda, and Cambodia, e.g.), basic stability was provided through a peace agreement. In other cases (Ethiopia and Eritrea), stability was created through a National Charter which provided for a basic structure of government and the guarantee of human rights which would govern the interim period while the Constitution was being created. In Eritrea, the Charter also had the advantage of providing considerable detail of how the process was to be conducted ruling on such questions as the creation of a Constitutional Commission and the election of a Constituent Assembly. In Poland a series of constitutional amendments served this purpose, and the most important among them—that of October 17, 1992 was referred to as the small constitution. The process in Hungary was similar in that interim arrangements were provided through constitutional amendment. An alternative model would provide for adoption of the constitution, with a constitutionally mandated review process—complete with the public participation component discussed below—following an interim period of three to five years.

South Africa enacted a formal Interim Constitution which served these purposes and set out a series of constitutional principles which were to guide the process. The structure of the Constitution-making process was determined by the South Africans themselves with minimal input from the international community. Prior to 1993, private negotiations amongst the various political factions in South Africa were important. But by 1993, the parties had negotiated an Interim Constitution which set out the basic ground rules for the process of adopting a permanent constitution and provided for the basic functioning of a Government of National Unity throughout the constitution-making period. Under the Interim Constitution, the final constitution was to be adopted by a Constituent Assembly on the basis of a two-thirds vote and no constitutional commission was created. Election to the Assembly was supervised by an Independent Electoral Commission and governed by a proportional representation list system laid out in the Interim Constitution. The Constituent Assembly, in addition to drafting a permanent constitution for the country, would also function as a parliament in the interim period. In addition, the Interim Constitution in South Africa set out 32 substantive principles which had to be followed in the drafting of the permanent constitution. Once the Constituent Assembly began to undertake the process of constitution-making, it determined that a comprehensive program of public participation was necessary. Public participation included publication of debates, consultations at the village level, radio broadcasts of public education material as well as key issues and large numbers of public submissions.

Most of these arrangements provided for some basic measures for the exercise of executive and legislative functions. In a few of the cases, there was provision for the exercise of interim judicial power to oversee the process. In South Africa, Poland, and Hungary, for example, the constitutional courts in those countries played this kind of an oversight role in connection with the constitution-making process. This role was particularly important in the South African context where the Interim Constitution also endowed the Constitutional Court with the jurisdiction to determine whether the final draft of the permanent constitution complied with the principles set out in the Interim Agreement. One draft was actually rejected by the Constitutional Court as inconsistent with the constitutional principles which had been established.

The interim arrangements are usually agreements formed amongst a broadly representative group of elites and do not involve public participation. In the South African case, the negotiations and settlement of the issues surrounding this initial stage of the process at that stage were closed and secretive, apparently due to concern over the high risk of violence at that stage. The constitution-making process has generally tended to be more closed and elite driven in those cases where the risk of violence is high; Cambodia serves as another example of this phenomenon.

Reducing the Monopoly of Power and Influence

While powerful elite factions will play a major role in any post-conflict constitution-making process, it is essential to reduce their monopolization of that process, and to avoid a final constitution that simply reflects division of the spoils between such factions. If the constitution and the process of its adoption are to play a role in transforming society, then constraints on such monopoly of power need to be built into the process.

One tool in this regard is allowing adequate time for the constitutional process. A rapidly adopted constitution will generally only reflect a deal between the powerful. A more open and extended process provides an opportunity for other groups and civil society in general to challenge and debate and influence the process: A second element is the adoption at the outset of a set of basic rules that will govern both the process of constitution-making and the substance of the ultimate document. These may include, for example, tolerance, pluralism, human rights, the rule of law, limited government, the role of the military constitutionally limited to defensive functions, and gender, religious and ethnic equality.[1] Both of these steps serve to

[1] Related to the notion of cardinal rules, there is a trend in modem constitutions to include certain substantive features which are considered so sacrosanct as to be impossible to amend under the terms of the Constitution. These features are sometimes referred to as "immutable principles." There does not seem to be as yet any consistency with respect to which principles are thus considered to be immutable. In Germany, human rights and the federal nature of the system are immutable, and in France, the republican form of government is immutable. In those countries which have constitutional courts with jurisdiction to resolve disputes over issues of constitutionality, the existence of these immutable principles raises the possibility that the court may be called upon to rule on the constitutionality of a proposed constitutional amendment.

constrain the ability of current power centers to drive the constitutional process in the wrong direction, and would be advisable in the case of Iraq.

Public Participation and Ownership

There is a clearly emerging trend toward providing for more direct participation by the population in the constitution-making process, in the form of civic education and popular consultation. Some scholars are referring to this as "new constitutionalism." This trend seems to have begun and emerged particularly in Africa although at this point in time it has also been employed in Latin America (Brazil and Nicaragua) and Asia (East Timor and Fiji.) Rather than being crafted completely behind closed doors by a small number of elites and handed down from on high, this model enables the broader public to be engaged in the process. It can serve to empower a broader range of groups, including women and emerging civil society groups, as examples, providing an opportunity for them to impact on the constitutional process as well as on the political process. The constitutional process can provide a forum for national dialogue and education regarding issues and decisions that are vital to the future direction of the country.

This model has typically involved the establishment of a Constitutional Commission as it did in Eritrea, Ethiopia, Ugandan, Kenya, Rwanda, Nicaragua, Brazil, and Fiji. Typically the Constitutional Commission has three functions although the delineation of those functions has not always been clear, and the lack of delineation has contributed to the weakness of the process in some cases, see below.

In general, Commissions have been called upon to conduct civic education in connection with the constitution-making process, to consult the population on the questions which it determines to be key to the process, and then to compile a draft of the Constitution which takes that consultation into account and which also synthesizes other drafts and submissions from political parties, individuals, and NGO's. This tends to diffuse the focus on individual drafts which can otherwise detract from the democracy of the process when ready-made drafts are submitted in the early stages of the process by powerful parties or individuals.

These Constitutional Commissions have usually been appointed by the executive or elected or appointed by a Constituent Assembly. In this new emerging model for constitution-making, it is important that such bodies, while relatively small in size, be fairly representative of the various political parties and religious, racial and ethnic groups within the society. Where the constitution-making process has been sufficiently deliberative and has entailed broad public consultation, an intriguing result has repeatedly been the transformation of the members of a Constitutional Commission from serving primarily as advocates for their respective interest group into a more cohesive group with a greater focus on the needs of the whole society.

Constitution-making is a deliberative process, and especially when integrating the public participation model, needs to be given adequate time. It is a mistake to attempt to short-circuit this process. For example, in some cases, Commissions have tried to conduct civic education and popular consultation all in one phase. It is strongly urged that these generally be treated as two distinct phases of the process. The public education phase provides an important vehicle to broadly disseminate to the public information regarding the constitution and the constitutional process, and information on the basic themes—that should inform the new constitutional framework. In various places, this has served as a stimulus to civil society groups to organize public discussions on these issues. Through this process, long before adoption of any final constitution, the process can begin to diffuse power within the society and facilitate democratization, rather than leaving it all in the hands of those few with their hands on the levers of power.

In East Timor and Fiji, the public education and consultation phases were essentially conflated, arguably weakening the effectiveness of each. South Africa, Eritrea, and Rwanda are more successful examples of this aspect of the process. In those processes, a carefully planned program of civic education was conducted so as to educate the population on the role of a constitution in society generally and as to their role in the process. Also, it was during the program of civic education that the determination was made as to what questions were the most important for the population. In Rwanda and Eritrea, the population was then consulted for their response on these questions. Over the course of the Rwandan constitutional process, it is worth noting, the opinions of the Constitutional Commission were revised in light of the popular consultations. Albania also provides a very useful model of a robust and well-organized public education and consultation process, which has arguably strengthened the drive toward democratization in that country.

During the public consultation phase, the Constitutional Commission should present to the population a series of specific key questions and issues regarding the constitution. An adequate budget and resources are needed to enable the Commission to hold sessions throughout the country, elicit the views of the public and compile and receive responses. This process not only provides the public with a sense of ownership over the future constitution; it also often provides ideas and insights to the Commission that may prove extremely valuable to the subsequent drafting of the constitutional text.

The case studies have clearly shown that the challenge of conducting these processes in the context of a high rate of illiteracy has proven to be much less significant than some would imagine. Members of constitutional commissions have been frequently amazed at the sophistication of the views expressed by their illiterate population once they understood the issues and were able to form their own opinions about them. In addition, a great deal has been learned about how to conduct these processes with art illiterate population. The message has been passed in several of these societies through the use of radio, cartoons, traveling theatrical presentations, etc.

The synthesis of the results of the popular consultation into the constitutional draft has been a challenge in certain cases, and requires proper planning. In East Timor, for example, the Constituent Assembly focused on a draft prepared by the dominant political party that ignored the results of the popular consultation. Brazil is another example where the popular consultation failed at this stage. In that case the popular consultation had been massive but poorly organized. The task of synthesizing the results was then assigned to one man. Consequently, he was ultimately unable to absorb and synthesize the results of the popular contribution in the development of the final draft.

It is also important to note that the process of civic education and popular consultation takes time. Some countries conducting these processes have tried to rush them. This was the case in East Timor, where the process was to take one month; a year later when the process was seen to have failed, the Constituent Assembly launched a second effort at public consultation, but allocated only one week for the exercise. This is currently a potential problem in Afghanistan is well. An effective public education and consultation process will take at least a year, and some countries have spent as much as three years on this aspect of the process.

Democratic Representation

In addition to public participation, an important factor for the ultimate legitimacy of the constitution and the stability of the system it establishes is democratic representation in the body that receives the Commission draft. This is often a Constituent Assembly that debates and revises the Commission draft and adopts the Constitution.

The case studies suggest that a broadly representative Constituent Assembly is more likely to adopt a constitution which is characterized as legitimate and to establish a political system which will prove to be stable. When there is broad democratic representation, there is a greater likelihood that all aggrieved parties will have an opportunity to express their views on key constitutional issues of importance to them, and perhaps more importantly, there is a greater likelihood that their views will be taken into consideration in the drafting of the final document. Where this is the case, the Constitution can serve to resolve conflict and provide mechanisms and reliable institutions for peaceful resolution of conflicts in the future.

The biggest problem that arises in this connection is the dominance of a single political party, and this problem has been encountered in many of the cases studied. It is a factor which frequently detracts from the democracy of the process and serves to block the resolution of issues which are important to minority groups who have historically felt aggrieved.

For this reason, frequently a great deal of thought is given to the choice of the electoral systems which will govern democratic representation, and very often an Electoral Commission is established to oversee the elections of the Constituent Assembly and to resolve conflicts which may arise in this connection.

A problem which frequently occurs in connection with the dominance of a particular party is the establishment of a constitutional draft early in the process which becomes the focus of all debate and discussion. This problem was observed recently in East Timor, for example, where the Fretilin party developed a proposed draft even before the constitution-making process was formally initiated. The disadvantage which stems from the early establishment of drafts by powerful parties or individuals is that debate then tends to focus on the power to be accorded to that group or individual rather than on the issues that the draft addresses. This phenomenon serves to make the process generally less democratic.

One way to combat this problem is to establish a Constitutional Commission charged with the functions described above in the section on the right to participate. In that case, the Commission can serve as the recipient of all drafts and other submissions from all parties and individuals. The Commission can then take those drafts and submissions into consideration along with the results of the popular consultation. They can then synthesize all of the elements in the final draft which they then prepare for submission to the Constituent Assembly for debate. This kind of a system can diffuse the power associated with any particular individual or group and provide an opportunity to all of the various groups in the society to express their views on constitutional issues.

Ratification

The case studies have not revealed any particularly uniform method for ratification of a Constitution. In many of the cases studied, the Constitution has been ratified by a Constituent Assembly elected for that purpose, and in several cases the Constitution had to be adopted by a ⅔ vote of that body. South Africa, Cambodia, and East Timor are examples. In other cases, the Constitution has been ratified simply by the parliament (Fiji, for example), in one case, Columbia, the Constitution was ratified by Presidential decree, and in Rwanda, the Constitution was ratified by popular referendum. It is interesting to note that there is a tradition of ratification by popular referendum in those countries, like Rwanda and earlier Iraq, which are influenced by the French Constitutional tradition.

However, none of the case studies has suggested any problems relating to legitimacy of the Constitution that can be traced to the method chosen for ratification. They suggest that questions of legitimacy appear to be more related to the education of the population and their participation in the process, as discussed above.

The Role of the International Community

At the outset, it is important to note that the role of the international community has been essential in many constitution-making exercises. For example, some of the programs of civic education and popular consultation which are described above could not have been conducted without the contribution of valuable resources from the international community. In addition, in virtually all of the cases studied, international constitutional experts have served as a valuable human resource to locals who have developed and drafted constitutions. The international community can play a role which is beneficial, and in some cases, crucial to the process.

The international community's involvement in constitutional processes has not always been without problems. For example, the role of the international community has been criticized in some cases for favoring one political party over others. When one party is allowed to dominate the process, there is a significant risk that aggrieved parties in a conflict will not have the opportunity to air their grievances and secure concessions in the constitution-making process which could serve to reduce the potential for future conflict. The problem is exacerbated when the international community lends its support to such a party.

The international community often engages in this kind of favoritism out of practical and temporal concerns. In general, their view is that it is perhaps most expedient to develop good working relations with the party which will obviously hold the power once the process is completed. In addition, there is the view that support of that party could shorten the process by accelerating an outcome which is seen as a forgone conclusion. This approach could, however, prove to be very short sighted in that, it could, as noted leave the embers of conflict smoldering.

This concern is related to another potential problem associated with the role of the international community in constitution-making processes—the issue of its influence on the timing of the process. The assistance of the international community to constitution-making is usually part of a larger program of rule of law assistance which is very demanding in terms of both human and financial resources. For this reason, the international community has frequently sought to expedite the process, and some have taken the view that this time pressure has served to short circuit the process in some cases. In Cambodia, for example, the Paris Peace Accords of 1991 provided that the constitution-making process should be completed in a period of ninety days. Analysts of this process have unanimously taken the view that this period was clearly too short, particularly given the lack of human resources resulting from the Cambodian genocide and the impossibility generally of conducting an effective process under such time constraints in the most ideal of circumstances. Some authorities have suggested that the rushed nature of the process contributed to the weakness of the system created under the Constitution of 1993, and the coup d'etat of 1997 has lent credence to that view.

Finally, while, as noted, the role of the international experts has been by and large extremely beneficial to the constitution-making processes studied, there have been instances where the contribution of certain individual experts has served to make the process less democratic. For example, in Cambodia while the process was unfolding in 1993 King Sihanouk commissioned a French expert to prepare his draft of the constitution. From the moment that draft was prepared, it then became more difficult for others participating in the process to make their views heard or to propose alternatives since from then on there was a tendency to reduce all issues to the question of whether the alternatives were consistent with the King's draft. (The problem associated with the development of drafts early in the process is more fully discussed earlier.) The study has shown that the role of foreign experts has been most constructive when they have served as a neutral resource offering guidance to locals by elucidating the pros and cons of particular substantive issues, frequently through comparative analysis of how constitutional issues have been handled in other countries. This kind of a role encourages debate of issues amongst the locals who will ultimately be the ones who will make the substantive choices. The making of informed choices by locals will serve to increase their sense of ownership of the constitution and contribute to its legitimacy in the long run. In Eritrea, an advisory body composed of foreign experts was created to assist the Eritrearts in this way.

Summary and Recommendations

The international community should encourage the Iraqis to take the time which is needed to conduct the process taking into consideration the time which will be required to engage in meaningful civic education and popular consultation.

Basic rules governing the constitution-making process and the drafting of the final constitutional document should be established at the outset of the process. These rules should mandate a robust process of public engagement and should enshrine fundamental rights in the new Iraqi society.

The case studies suggest that Iraq should follow the new model of constitutionalism which is emerging in recent constitution-making exercises by taking steps to ensure that meaningful civic education and popular consultation are conducted. In order to accomplish this goal, a Constitutional Commission should be appointed which is broadly representative of all of the political, religious, and ethnic factions within the society. This Commission could be appointed by the interim authority in Iraq as long as it is thus broadly representative of the society.

The Constitutional Commission should conduct its work in three separate phases. It should first engage in a program of civic education which informs the population of the role of the constitution in the society and lets its people know what will be expected of them during the popular consultation phase. During this phase, the Commission should be taking note of the values and issues which the society considers to be of paramount importance and should be compiling a list of specific questions which should be put to the population during the popular consultation phase.

In the second phase, the Commission should conduct consultations based upon specific questions, and these consultations should take place in every area of the country in both rural and urban settings. The Commission should also receive submissions and proposed drafts from political parties, individuals and NGO's.

In the third phase of its work, the Commission should develop a draft which synthesizes the results of the popular consultation and the other submissions.

The interim authority should develop an electoral law which should establish the electoral system which should be used in the election of a Constituent Assembly and which will provide for the establishment of a broadly representative Electoral Commission which will supervise the election and resolve disputes which arise during the election.

The Constituent Assembly should carefully consider and debate every article in the draft proposed by the Constitutional Commission. It should be empowered in the electoral law to adopt the Constitution by a two thirds vote of the Assembly.

It would be useful for the international community to provide detailed advice to the Iraqis on the development of the constitution-making process. As noted above, in the past foreign experts have focused almost exclusively on issues of substance. In a place like Iraq, locals could greatly benefit from an analysis of lessons learned from other processes which could serve to ensure the legitimacy of the Constitution and the stability of the political system it creates.

International experts should serve as a resource and should avoid acting as a "hired gun" for particular parties or groups within Iraq. They should offer comparative observations based on their knowledge of how particular constitutional issues have been dealt with in other countries.

The international community should avoid supporting one group or political party over another.

Senator CORNYN. Thank you very much. I just have a couple of questions. To start with, Dr. Kommers, the issue of de-Ba'athification arose with the first panel, and I know after World War II in Germany there was a de-Nazification effort. Can you perhaps tell us whether you think that experience should enlighten us today on the de-Ba'athification process, and specifically if people are excluded from society, or from holding government jobs, what that portends for a successful democracy?

Dr. KOMMERS. Yes, there was a major de-Nazification program in Germany. However, as I think somebody suggested from the previous panel, the members of the Nazi Party came in various stripes. At the worst end, of course, you had the criminals, and those who had been guilty of criminal activity for the most part were barred from public office and from all positions of responsibility in post war Germany.

As was said before in connection with the Ba'ath Party there were thousands of people who belonged to the Nazi Party, but who joined the party simply, for example, to retain their jobs in the government bureaucracy, which of course was extremely large, as it is today, and by the way, the same process took place in East Germany.

Almost all East German communists who were high in the echelons of the Socialist Unity Party, the Communist Party were discharged or removed from office. These included political officials, teachers, judges, and civil servants. But those people who could show that they were not associated with the crimes of the regime were allowed to retain or reclaim their positions. This was a good policy because it contributed to some degree of trust and it also contributed to the stability, such as it was, in East Germany immediately after reunification, in the 2 or 3 years after reunification, and I think the same was true of the post-Nazi period.

The lower level Nazi officials who really were not ideologically committed to the regime, and there were many, although that's disputed, if they had been left out of account, I think it would have created a good deal of unhappiness and distrust in Germany, and then finally the Americans, as well as the British and the French, realized that many of these officials were absolutely necessary if the government was to be adequately staffed and reconstructed.

Senator CORNYN. Thank you.

Professor Agawa, when your people question where democracy and Islam can coexist, I think about the seismic cultural change in Japan post-World War II, particularly with regard to the role of the Emperor, and I wonder if you might enlighten us a little bit in terms of the role of the Emperor in Japan pre-World War II and through the war, and how that changed during the course of the constitution of Japan.

Mr. AGAWA. In talking about the Japanese constitution in 1946, as I said, the question as to how to treat the Emperor in that constitution was a major issue at the time. We have to remember that the Emperor tradition goes back to the third century or fourth century, and the Emperor is much older than any constitutional system we know, and when the Americans proposed that the Emperor be just a mere symbol of the unity of the people, the sovereignty resides with the people, and that any power that the Emperor has is derived from the people's sovereignty, the Japanese people, particularly the conservative government element really strongly resisted that.

However, actually, then they later found out that the tradition of the Emperor, going back to the 9th, 17th, and even oldest period, the Emperor was really just a spiritual symbol, and the Emperor being a militaristic superpower was only an adaption of the so-called Prussian German notion of Kaiser during the late 19th century, and particularly during the thirties.

So therefore in a very interesting way the notion of a democratic Emperor suited the older tradition of Japanese history, and I think that in that way the 1946 constitutional notion of spiritual symbol of Japan has worked remarkably well, so I think in that respect General MacArthur was very wise in bringing up that notion, and modeled after that partly on I think the British way of reigning but not ruling monarchy.

Senator CORNYN. Professor Howard, I was interested in your comments in this vein. We are very cognizant, and there is almost universal agreement that the coalition should not impose our views on the Iraqi people, it must be something of their choosing, yet you talked about the importation of values, and indeed it seems to me that the failure of any Iraqi constitution to respect certain basic values would be dangerous to the Iraqi people, in other words, if there is not respect for freedom of the press, free exercise of religion, sovereignty of the people and those sorts of things. Could you address that?

It seems to me like we are defensive in not wanting to impose something, and yet if they don't embrace some of those certain values which I think are pretty universal in a civilized world now, not just America, it could indeed perpetuate a police state, or set up a situation where another Saddam could rise to power. Do you have thoughts?

Mr. HOWARD. I think that's a core question. It seems to me that we must accept the proposition, which has been widely accepted at these two panels, that of course the Iraqi people must be at the core of the enterprise. I mean, they must be the ones who make, devise, institute, implement the constitution. We all understand that, but I think one need not be defensive about saying that there are certain values which transcend national boundaries.

We've had so much experience—Neil Kritz and his associates and a number of other people have studied much of this experience, especially in the years since World War II. I would hazard that a majority of the constitutions of the world have been written in the last 25 or 30 years. There's really been no period like it since the American founding period, or perhaps the period after World Wars I and II. There is ample opportunity for seeing whether, indeed, there is common ground among constitution-makers.

This approach is not unlike the effort of Enlightenment thinkers in the 18th century, Voltaire, Condorcet, Turgot, and others, who argued that there was what Condorcet called a "common core of human happiness." One should take account of national differences; no two peoples are alike. Yet when one strips away those national differences, there are certain human aspirations and appetites, pains and pleasures, which make us all human beings. That, it seems to me, is the heart and soul of the modern human rights movement.

In Vienna, a few years ago, there was a meeting at the United Nations that came together to talk about the meaning of human rights. There was a handful of nations who objected to the enterprise, nations like China and Burma. I had the impression that those nations had not consulted their people as to whether there was such a thing as human rights.

So I, for one, am willing to begin with a certain a priori assumption that there are certain rights that people ought to have as a matter of principle, and that constitution-makers, no matter who they are, ought to address those rights.

I would perhaps distinguish between what we call bills of rights, where you lay out the rights of individuals, and the structural side of government, the frame of government. Surely there's a much wider room for debate—shall the system be parliamentary or Presidential, shall we have an American-style Supreme Court or a German-style constitutional court? If there's a president, shall he or she be a figurehead or a president with some power like France or the United States?

There are many models from which to choose from, it seems to me. Even as to structure, however, there are some presumptive basic qualities. I mentioned them in my remarks—norms like separation of powers, checks and balances, judicial review or other enforceability of the constitution. All of these are working models. What one does then is take stock of how different countries have used them and hope that, perhaps doing a little nudging, that the Iraqis, when they finally write their constitution, will properly have taken stock of that experience.

Senator CORNYN. Thank you. Senator Chafee.

Senator CHAFEE. Thank you very much, Senator.

Professor Kommers, you mentioned that the German constitutional basic law has been a model, if I heard you right, for 60 or 65 countries, and rather strong on that as perhaps applicable to Iraq. Are any of those 60 or 65 countries that have any similarity to Iraq? I don't know which 60 or 65, if I heard you right, they are.

Dr. KOMMERS. Well, most of the Eastern European constitutions were revised at last partially on the German model. The same is true of South Africa's constitution, and the Spanish constitution, the Portuguese constitution, a couple of the new constitutions in Latin America, but I can't think of—well, maybe Bosnia, Bosnia-Herzegovina, where you have tribalism and religious radicalism being present pretty much as in the case of Iraq, and I'm really not sure how well those constitutions are working. I suspect that they are not working as well as the drafters of those constitutions wanted them to work.

Maybe along the same lines, Mr. Chafee, I might mention another reason why I think the German constitution has been so successful which may have lessons for Iraq, and that is this. The main parties in the German constitutional convention represented the three major democratic traditions in the history of Germany. There was the Christian Democratic, the socialist tradition, and the liberal tradition, represented respectively by the Christian Democratic Union, the Social Democratic Party, and the Free Democratic Party. These represent the major historical and philosophical movements that are part of Germany's liberal democratic tradition.

These parties had their differences, and they fought out those differences bitterly at the convention, but in the end they suppressed those differences, and took the best of the three traditions and incorporated those things into the basic law, so if you look at that basic law, it represents something of a confluence of these three traditions in German history.

Then finally, the last point, Adenauer. Adenauer was elected the president of the constitutional convention. He was Germany's Washington. He was a towering figure, highly respected not only by the Germans but by the allies, and I'm just wondering, if a constitutional convention of that kind is established in Iraq, that convention should probably represent the three or four major democratic traditions, if they exist in Iraq, and be governed, or ruled, or directed by people of reputation and prestige, it seems to me, and then maybe the Americans can direct that process, at least to some extent.

Senator CHAFEE. Thank you very much, and thank you very much, panelists, for your generous time here this afternoon.

Senator CORNYN. Senator Feingold.

Senator FEINGOLD. Thank you, Mr. Chairman.

Professor Yoo, you and many of the other witnesses have suggested, in order to create a stable, lasting order in Iraqi, the Iraqi people have to be the primary authors of their own constitution and political order. You apparently believe we have the legal authority to impose a constitution on the Iraqi people. Are you suggesting it would be a good idea for us to do so?

Mr. YOO. Thank you for that question.

No, I'm not. I'm just stating that the law would allow you to do that, but I think the German and Japanese models actually show where, even though the United States had such broad legal authority they used domestic processes to help develop a constitution that would be acceptable to their own populations, but you know, especially with the Japanese example there was a very strong American hand. It was sort of based on this theory of international law of occupation that I discussed before. They just weren't so open about what they did.

Senator FEINGOLD. OK. Mr. Kritz, Mr. Yoo has testified that he believes the United States has the legal authority to impose a constitution on the Iraqi people. Do you agree?

Mr. KRITZ. Well, Senator, I think that current-day interpretation of the Hague Convention and Fourth Geneva Convention obligations, at least according to many scholars, would raise questions with respect to that. There is at a minimum a healthy controversy on the issue.

More importantly, I would suggest that on a practical basis, as Mr. Yoo has said as well, it wouldn't be a good move, simply because, in the context of Iraq, it would not provide for a product or a process that would move Iraq to the place where we want it to be at the end of this process.

Senator FEINGOLD. Let me followup with you. I think one of the themes emerging from this hearing is that when we're talking about drafting a constitution, process is just as important as content. We've heard a bit about the historical experiences of Japan and Germany, which are obviously important, but as you've mentioned, you've had experience with the more recent transitions in Bosnia, Cambodia, Rwanda, Sierra Leone, Guatemala and elsewhere. Based on your experience with these other countries, what would you say were the most important process issues we should be keeping in mind?

Mr. KRITZ. Well, as I indicated, Senator, one of the most important issues with respect to process is the guarantee of public participation and ownership of the process. The constitutional process, if it's going to be viable and create a reconciled and stable Iraq for the future, can't be a process of a few elites crafting a constitution behind closed doors and handing it down like tablets from Sinai.

This needs to be a process that really engages the people. It needs to be a process that includes several stages, including the initial process of articulation of basic principles. I would suggest, by the way, Senator Cornyn, that that notion of essential values is ensconced in several recent constitutional processes in the context of international human rights. This has been done recently in Afghanistan, as it has been done in other cases, and establishes a commitment that the country in its transition and its constitutional process is obliged to adhere to current international human rights norms. This helps ensure that the kinds of values and the protection of rights that we're talking about are obligatory on that process.

A constitutional commission should ideally be a representative body that would include respected and credible scholars from various key groups within society. It would engage first in public education on these principles, in consultation with respect to the public's ideas on basic questions, allowing them to engage in the debate, and only then in the drafting of a document.

One of the things that we've seen in a handful of cases is the immediate tabling of a document, frequently one that's been drafted by one dominant party in the process, and that immediately skews the entire constitutional process which follows. We've seen that in Cambodia; we've seen it to some extent in East Timor more recently. It makes it harder for that fuller democratic process to ensue. It makes more sense later on for the constitutional commission, based on its consultations and based on its input both from outside and inside the country to begin that process of crafting a document, which would then be submitted either to a popular referendum and/or to a constituent assembly for final revisions and adoption.

Senator FEINGOLD. Finally, Mr. Kritz, one of the biggest concerns in Iraq will be the creation of a criminal justice system that the Iraqi people perceive is fair and evenhanded. What are some of the problems that you see in places like East Timor and Kosovo with establishing new courts and police forces, where many of the people employed in the new criminal justice system are the same people who held the position before the change in government took place?

Mr. KRITZ. Senator, there would, of course, initially need to be, as has been discussed, this process of vetting those personnel who may populate the new system. I would mention, by the way, that the Institute of Peace, based on experience in a number of prior transitions, provided to the NSC Working Group on Iraq back in January a set of guidelines for the vetting process. I'd be pleased to provide a copy of that memo for the record, if you desire.

It will be necessary, as I say, initially to screen out many of the people who are currently in the system. That doesn't mean, in the Iraqi context, that everyone is discredited. Far from it. Within the police force, as the Iraqi Special Forces, Interior and others assumed greater power over the years under Saddam, the regular police forces actually became increasingly isolated, and that meant that they were not playing the dominant role in day-to-day abuses of the regime.

As a consequence, as I think the coalition forces have recognized, many of those police officers actually can be retrained and placed on the force. They will, however, need significant international assistance. One of the things that we're seeing today is the difficulty and the time-consuming process for the coalition forces of recruiting civilian police advisors from various allied countries in significant enough numbers to actually spread around a country of this size, and to reestablish the police forces.

Within the courts as well, many of the judges need retraining, but again, to the extent that they were not part of the security court apparatus, have the ability and the credibility to remain on the bench, with that retraining.

One of the lessons that has emerged from many of the cases of prior transitions over the last couple of decades is simply the need to recognize that this is going to take a long time. Recreating a legal culture, changing the way courts and police and prison officials function is not going to happen in 6 months or a year. It's going to take a number of years.

It's going to take substantial resources for training. It's going to take substantial resources for oversight and monitoring. It will probably require the insertion of international advisors, if not in an executive authority fashion as we've seen in Kosovo and East Timor, then at a minimum at the courts, at the police stations, at the prisons, with the ability to oversee and keep an eye and inform the process as it goes forward.

The last point that I would mention is the imperative of dealing with the question of the major crimes of the past regime. The entire process of re-standing up their criminal justice system won't have credibility in the eyes of the Iraqi people if this issue isn't addressed as well, and on this last point, it will require several tiers of activity.

The major war crimes cases, I would submit, can only be undertaken with substantial international involvement and participation in a special tribunal for major crimes. Whether that's a hybrid tribunal that includes both Iraqis and outsiders—and I would advocate that over any kind of a wholly internationalized process, again for the reasons of ownership we've discussed—that will only touch the tip of the iceberg. Separate from major crimes under international law, like crimes against humanity, there will be large numbers of cases that will be heard for regular crimes in the Iraqi criminal courts, and those will need to be monitored carefully.

Last, in addition to the vetting and trials, there is arguably a role for the truth and reconciliation process that was mentioned in the prior panel. This can allow a larger number of Iraqis to deal with these abuses in ways that the courts will never be able to, and to come together, as was done in South Africa and elsewhere, to examine how these things happened, and to develop a blueprint for what kinds of responses are appropriate—both in terms of penalizing and memorializing the past as well as in terms of steps for the future to build a structure in which these abuses cannot recur.

Senator FEINGOLD. I thank the panel. I thank both the chairmen very much.

Senator CORNYN. Thank you, Senator Feingold. Senator Chafee, do you have any further questions?

Miraculously we were able to complete our second panel without being interrupted for votes. That probably means a late night for us, but that's all right. At least we were able to get through the testimony of the witnesses.

I want to thank the members of the second panel, as I did the first, for your testimony both oral and in writing, your written statements. I think today's hearing has helped fill a very significant void, and hopefully we'll begin a certain conversation that I think needs to take place about this very important subject, one that will hopefully give democracy an opportunity to begin, once we secure the countryside and establish the rule of law and some independent judiciary, but this has been a very important contribution to that effort. I want to congratulate and thank each one of you.

I want to thank certainly the chairman of my full committee, Senator Hatch, and obviously the chairman of the Senate Foreign Relations Committee, on which both Senator Feingold and Senator Chafee serve, for their help. I want to tell Senator Chafee and Senator Feingold how much I appreciate their cooperation, as well as that of their staff. As always, it's the staff that does all the heavy lifting, and I want to express publicly my appreciation to all of our staff for the good work that they've done to make today's hearing possible.

Finally, let me just close by saying that again, if there's any other documents that anyone would like to make part of the record, we'll leave the record open till July 2, and it could be that members of the panel, even those who were not able to be here physically today, would like to submit additional questions in writing, and I hope you would be open to that.

With that, let me say thank you very much, and the hearing is now adjourned.

[Whereupon, at 4:39 p.m., the hearing was adjourned.]

APPENDIX

TRANSITIONAL JUSTICE IN POST-SADDAM IRAQ

The Road to Re-establishing Rule of Law and Restoring Civil Society

A Blueprint [1]

I. EXECUTIVE OVERVIEW

BACKGROUND

The Working Group on Transitional Justice of the Future of Iraq Project (Working Group), in cooperation with the Iraqi Jurists' Association, commenced the development of this Transitional Justice Project in meetings starting in July of 2002.

Comprised primarily of prominent former Iraqi judges, lawyers and law professors, the Working Group embarked on this project in consultation with international experts in the areas of international criminal law, truth and reconciliation, post-conflict justice and military reform.

These jurists came together with a common purpose and a singular objective. The common purpose was to assert that in order to achieve civil society in a future post-Saddam Iraq, it must be founded on the principle of respect for the rule of law. Their singular objective has been to identify and document the necessary procedures, mechanisms, rules and laws to initiate the transformation of Iraq to a society governed by the rule of law.

PREMISE

There are two primary aspects for the concept of the rule of law. The first is that all persons are accountable under the law regardless of their rank or position in the country, including the head of state. The second is to provide the citizens a credible means to address legitimate grievances and to avoid self-help justice characterized by acts of vengeance.

At the outset, it was universally recognized that the foundation for a society governed by the rule of law is an independent judiciary. By contrast, the government of Saddam Hussein went to great lengths to subvert each of the major powers of state (ie. legislative, judiciary and executive) to the central authority of the president through the Ba'ath party apparatus.

The role of an independent judiciary cannot be over-emphasized, particularly in a society where individual rights and freedoms have been trampled upon so comprehensively as they have been in Iraq under Saddam Hussein.

VISION FOR THE FUTURE

The vision of the Working Group for a future Iraq is one founded on the notion that the laws and institutions of state must be restructured and reformed to serve and protect the interests of its citizens. This is in stark contrast to Saddam's practice of manipulating every instrument and agency of state to protect and serve his regime. In order to re-establish civil society in Iraq, there must be a clear departure from the past and a clear focus placed on the welfare of the Iraqi people.

---

[1] Report of the Working Group on Transitional Justice in Iraq, and Iraqi Jurists' Association (March 2003). A complete copy of the report, which contains appended material not printed as part of this hearing transcript, has been placed in the committee's permanent files.

II. Transitional Justice Plan

This Transitional Justice Plan is aimed at transforming an unstable and chaotic state, caused by a dictatorship with a legacy of gross human rights abuses, to a democratic pluralistic system which respects the rule of law.

Transitional justice in the context of Iraq today demands sincere efforts to create the environment of trust and confidence in a new system, particularly a judicial system which establishes the rule of law in all of its meanings. This includes the general public's respect and confidence in the legal system to resolve disputes, prosecute crimes and also the important task of holding all people accountable regardless of rank or position.

In the case of Saddam Hussein's regime, the prolonged, widespread use of terror and violence against the Iraqi people requires a systematic and comprehensive approach to transitional justice. Such an approach will necessarily have to deal with the past crimes of the regime as well as to proactively create the environment for a future which respects the rights of all Iraqi citizens with coherent laws and reformed institutions.

Addressing the regime's crimes through open and fair trials for those suspected of war crimes, crimes against humanity and other serious abuses is a cornerstone of this plan. In addition, Truth Committees with a mandate to discover the truth, establish a record and disseminate this information on the national and international levels are proposed. Victims' compensation mechanisms are recommended as a key element in the effort to inhibit potential public demands for vengeance.

Building a future on the basis of respect for the rule of law requires a thorough review of the system of laws left behind by this regime to identify, remove and/or replace those provisions which violate internationally recognized basic human, civil and political rights. Beyond reforming the laws, major reforms are also required for key institutions to re-establish their roles to protect and serve the public in contrast to their current capacity to protect and serve the regime of Saddam Hussein.

In parallel with these reforms and the truth, accountability and reconciliation processes, a far-reaching program to educate and re-train professionals in various fields is needed to promote basic values of public service and protection of individual rights. An additional component to the education program is to raise public awareness of the essential rights and responsibilities of citizens building a civil society in all spheres of life, including schools, colleges, the media and other public forums for the long-term transformation of the institutions and society in general.

The following sections are concrete recommendations and draft laws in each of these important areas:

A. DEALING WITH THE PAST

It may be impossible for Iraqis to confidently and boldly face the challenges of an uncertain future, without first taking a hard, sober look at the past decades under Saddam's rule and thereafter directly addressing the fallout from the widespread crimes and repressive policies which are the hallmark of his regime. Re-establishing the rule of law and preventing individuals or groups from resorting to mob-justice requires a genuine, meaningful process to identify, prosecute and hold perpetrators of crimes accountable for their actions.

Beyond the major crimes, an active truth and reconciliation process is required to identify, record and disseminate information about what transpired under this regime. Additional remedies other than deprivation of liberty such as personal payment of victims' compensation, community service and lustration mechanisms are available for those offenses which do not rise to the level of major crimes.

1. Truth, Accountability and Reconciliation

a. Prosecution v. Truth Committees

The Iraqi regime's crimes against humanity are some of the worst in world history. Although, they have been amply recorded, they are extremely difficult to quantify with any precision.

Having established this fact, it remains necessary to give hope even to some of the perpetrators of less serious abuses. This may be done by a plea bargain offering amnesty for those who defect, or expose the regime's crimes and the persons involved. Such an offer can be made pursuant to law No. 23 of 1971 of the Criminal Procedure Code. (Note—all code references refer to the Iraqi legal codes unless specifically indicated otherwise) Article 29 of this law states:

1. The investigative judge may offer amnesty with the approval of the criminal court for reasons set forth on the record in the case against any person accused of wrong doing with a view to obtaining their testimony against other perpetrators provided said accused presents a complete, truthful account. If

the offer is accepted, the testimony shall be heard and the accused shall retain his/her status until a verdict is reached in the case.

2. If the accused does not present a complete, truthful account, he/she shall lose his/her right to amnesty by decision of the criminal court.
3. If the court finds that the account presented by the accused offered the amnesty is complete and truthful, it will cease all criminal proceedings and release said accused pursuant to the terms of the amnesty.

Tenets of the Islamic law may also be used in this connection, especially those that allow the victim or the victim's relatives to forfeit their rights against the perpetrator upon reconciliation, in an act of Forgiveness.

However, it must be made clear to all Iraqis that the law shall be firmly and severely applied against those who resort to score-settling or vengeful acts irrespective of their status. The point must be emphasized that the principles of transitional justice shall be uniformly enforced against offenders in fair trials where the deserving parties shall be justly compensated for damages.

b. Truth Committees

There is a strong link between truth and reconciliation committees and the qualified amnesty of certain crimes to be later defined.

The truth and reconciliation committees are set up and their functions are defined by order of a judicial council. They are to do everything necessary to reveal the truth with regard to abuses that do not amount to international or major crimes. These lesser abuses may be so numerous that they cannot be prosecuted by courts of law. (A case in point is Rwanda where more than 400,000 people were implicated in such abuses, and their prosecution would have taken hundreds of years.) The measures in question would involve admission of guilt. That is why the aim of these committees is to arrive at the truth and consequently at the higher objective of reconciliation.

For the truth committees to attain their goals, they need to do the following:

1. Investigate claims formally and publicly reveal the truth about past human rights violations and the individuals involved.
2. Contribute to justice by imposing sentences other than deprivation of liberty, including amnesty for crimes covered by such a move, compensation for damages. In the event the case involves crimes beyond its jurisdiction or there is a breach of amnesty conditions, it shall refer the case to the criminal investigation committees which in turn may send the accused to a court of competent jurisdiction.
3. Induce confessions of responsibility and guilt. Reconciliation and amnesty is thus not tantamount to acquittal.
4. Involve and satisfy the concerns of victims, achieve reconciliation and renounce vengeance, vendettas and violence.
5. Link amnesty to the work of truth committees in bringing about reconciliation. Amnesty shall not extend to those who do not confess responsibility for abuses and publicly apologize for their misdeeds. This is similar to what occurred in South Africa.

Decisions of these committees must be subject to appeal. The truth committees should also have the power to take such decisions in addition to imposing sentences not involving imprisonment.

In each Appeals Court District, one or more truth and reconciliation committees may be set up as required. They are to comprise three members headed by a judicial officer. The members must be qualified and known for their integrity and good reputation in the community.

c. Reconciliation Mechanisms

To bring about reconciliation and to encourage people toward acceptance, tolerance and compassion rather than vengeance, structures must be in place that are in accord with local traditions, customs and norms.

The reconciliation project is important and its objective is to promote a favourable climate for normal life in a society that has been stunted by dictatorship. It is designed to help society move forward towards stability and democratic transformation.

A large number of people will likely be implicated in abuses due to the nature of Saddam's contradictory and complex policies which required individuals to demonstrate their loyalty to the regime by transgressing on the rights of others. To punish this huge number of abuses, assuming the necessary possibilities are available to do that, is to risk undermining the existing social and economic set-up threatening the state itself. This is why the work undertaken in implementing the transitional justice and reconciliation project is so essential. It, therefore, requires technically oriented individuals who are committed to a pluralistic, democratic society which respects the rule of law.

The main objectives in a reconciliation process that can assure the uniform dispensation of justice and set the foundation for the rule of law are:

1. Build confidence in the new administration and cooperation with it. This may be realized through the following:

   Granting special priority to the issue of compensation. Fair and just compensation should be granted to victims without discrimination. Failing to do so will invite resentment, protest and eventually rebellion if the issue is manipulated by opponents of the new administration. Moreover, a fair settlement of this issue will help victims overcome their vengeful impulses towards the perpetrators and their relatives. Compensation is a pivotal element of reconciliation.

   Raising the standard of living for civil servants. Conditions for living a decent life have been denied Iraqis under Saddam's regime. A nation-wide drive will be required to raise the standard of living, particularly of civil servants, as a guard against social corruption, thereby attacking its economic causes. This will help maintain self-interests within the accepted moral norms and remove any contradiction between private and public interests.

   Establishing legal safeguards to deter the new administration from imposing restrictions on individual freedoms. To rule out any form of authoritarianism in a post-Saddam Iraq, institutions and structures with appropriate checks and balances must be in place. Above all is the requirement for an independent judiciary. The more independent the judiciary is, the more just and effective it will be.

2. Highlight those tenets of Islamic law (Shari'a) that emphasize virtue, tolerance and forgiveness. Use may be made of early Islamic experiences which applied the principles of piety, justice, honesty, tolerance and respect for differences rather than ethnic, sectarian, religious, class or clan discrimination as practiced by Saddam's regime and the Ba'ath party. People need to be reminded that Islam could not have built a vast empire in its heyday if it had not espoused justice and virtue as its foundation. This policy will effectively contribute to preventing score-settling and vendettas in the wake of regime change.

3. Make use of traditional conventions and structures like tribal values to maintain order and ward off anarchy in the interests of reconciliation. This is despite the fact that these tribal values were encouraged by prior repressive regimes, nonetheless, they need to be acknowledged in the transition to a pluralist system and may even be a useful vehicle for enfranchisement of otherwise disenfranchised individuals or groups.

d. Prosecution

Holding Saddam Hussein and his cohorts responsible for their crimes against the Iraqi people requires prosecution under Iraqi penal codes. The salient issues in this regard are:

(i) Legal Basis for Prosecution

How to serve out arrest warrants.

How to conduct the investigation and file charges.

How to address the question of immunity granted to Iraqi officials under the existing constitution.

(ii) Court Structure

Which courts shall hear which types of cases?

(i) Legal Basis for Prosecution

Iraqi law No. 23, 1971 of the Criminal Procedure Code sets forth the nature of the proceedings relevant to criminal cases. Article 1 states that it is permissible to set a criminal case in motion by an oral or written complaint presented to an investigative judge, a prosecutor or a competent official at a police station. Such a case can also be initiated by an "Information" presented to the public prosecutor. On the basis of this Information, an investigation is opened. The investigative judge shall take such necessary steps as issuing a summons, search warrants and arrest warrants against the suspect(s). In the case of arrest warrants, the accused shall be described in detail by name, title, identification (card/number), physical description, place of residence, occupation, the type of alleged offense, the relevant penal code and date of the warrant.

The question then becomes, in the event there is no complaint filed against an official, particularly in the event there is a coup or an occupation by outside forces, can the investigative judge serve an arrest warrant and determine the nature of the suspect's custody/detention based merely on suspicion?

The answer is yes. Article 103 of the Criminal Procedure Code allows the arrest of any person suspected on reasonable grounds of having committed a major crime or an intentional felony without the need for a formal complaint. Precedent shows such suspects have been put under arrest by investigative judges pending inquiry into their alleged crime or involvement in a criminal act. Investigative judges can invoke this provision to arrest and question state officials without an initial summons or complaint being formally lodged against them.

As for the legal mechanism required to serve these arrest warrants, it is proposed that a Judicial Council be established, comprised of at least 9 members selected from judges forcibly retired in Iraq, those in exile and others presently in the Kurdish region. This Council can serve as a nucleus of the judiciary in a post-Saddam Iraq, expanding to include judges of integrity inside Iraq, after regime change. The Council shall have all the powers of the judiciary as defined in the future interim constitution or basic law.

The Judicial Council shall select a presiding judge who may be the same person as the presiding judge of the Cassation Court. The Council shall appoint investigative judges to investigate alleged crimes by officials of Saddam's regime under the Iraqi penal code. The Council shall also serve to vet members of the judiciary with authority to retire judges with questionable political backgrounds or integrity. Vacancies created by such actions may be filled by recalling retired judges of sound character and lawyers known for their competence. The Judicial Council may assume its constitutional and legal duties in the interests of justice during the transitional period.

It is proposed to initially confine all arrest warrants to top officials of the regime, including its head, his immediate associates, deputies, Revolutionary Command Council (RCC) members, ministers, regional leadership members, heads of security agencies, army chief of staff and corps commanders.

(ii) Court Structure

Special Courts for International and Major Crimes

Criminal trials by no means imply automatic conviction of the accused. They are legal proceedings designed to arrive at the truth. The accused is innocent until proven guilty. These trials shall be instrumental in revealing the truth and eliminating the impulses for vengeance and violence. In this sense they are an effective contribution to transitional justice. The truth will lead either to conviction of the accused when proven guilty or to acquittal or to dismissal for lack of evidence.

Before holding criminal trials competent investigative teams, presided over by investigative judges, should be in place. They are to investigate officials suspected of war crimes, genocide, torture and crimes against humanity. There is no statute of limitations for the prosecution of these crimes, nor are they covered by any amnesty. The investigation teams should be supported by international experts while making use of facilities offered by specialized institutes to uncover and preserve incriminating evidence and other areas of expertise.

The measures taken by these teams are governed by provisions of the 1971 Criminal Procedure Code in line with all subsequent procedures by courts applying the same law. The investigation teams may present the respective cases to investigative judges for the issuance of arrest warrants, summons, and search warrants pursuant to the above-mentioned law. Alternatively, investigative judges may preside over these teams to facilitate the task of issuing the appropriate court orders.

Crimes not falling in the international crimes category specified above but covered under Iraqi penal codes may be investigated in the typical manner with magistrates. There may be a pressing need to increase the number of competent prosecutors to investigate these crimes due to their large number.

Criminal courts in Iraq are classified according to the nature and gravity of the crime. There are criminal courts dealing with offences punishable by more than five years in prison. There are misdemeanor courts that deal with offences carrying a maximum penalty of five-year imprisonment.

Saddam Hussein and his top officials will be tried for crimes that do not fall under either of the above two categories. Theirs are grave international acts involving war crimes, genocide, torture and crimes against humanity. There is neither a statute of limitation nor amnesty for these crimes.

Saddam Hussein and other officials at the highest echelons are to be indicted for three types of crimes:

1. The first are grave international crimes that come under international criminal law.
2. The second are major crimes codified in the Iraqi penal code.
3. The third are lesser crimes and offenses covered by Iraqi penal code.

(The third type is addressed in the section on truth and reconciliation committees.)

As for the first type, they are crimes that can be dealt with by one of the following:

An ad hoc international criminal court like those set up for former Yugoslavia and Rwanda. The maximum penalty that can be meted out by these courts is life imprisonment. They are formed by a resolution of the UN Security Council. (Note: the newly created International Criminal Court is unfortunately not an appropriate venue to prosecute these crimes as its mandate is limited to crimes committed after July 2002. The vast majority of crimes committed in Iraq occurred well before this date.)

A hybrid criminal court consisting of Iraqi and international judges. This court, too, would be set up by a UN Security Council resolution, and it may also be barred from passing sentences involving the death penalty in accordance with the provisions of the UN resolution. Such a resolution is likely to be consistent with the provisions of international criminal law, which was the case with the Yugoslavia and Rwanda courts.

A special national criminal court comprised of Iraqi judges according to law No 23 of 1971 on Criminal Procedure Code. It may be made up of a presiding judge and two associates who can seek counsel from international experts or have international judges acting as experts. The overwhelming majority of Iraqi jurists are in favour of this kind of court as it will ensure that the trials have a national character and forestall any criticism from local, Arab and regional quarters. The difficulty this court might encounter is related to the fact that under the most recent applications of international criminal law, the maximum penalty for these crimes has been life-imprisonment. The maximum sentence under the Iraqi penal code, however, is death for major crimes such as pre-meditated murder. It would be gravely unjust to prosecute murderers with the possibility of a death sentence, while war criminals and persons accused of crimes against humanity face only a life-sentence. One solution to this dilemma would be to allow for the use of the death penalty for those convicted of one or more of the four major international crimes. Another solution would be to have the appropriate/legitimate legislative body abolish capital punishment in the Iraqi penal code to be consistent with the recent applications of international law.

Domestic Criminal Courts

The second type of crimes is covered under the Iraqi penal code. With over 34 years of Ba'ath rule in Iraq, numerous and heinous crimes have been perpetrated. The number of perpetrators may run into the tens of thousands. These crimes come under the jurisdiction of Iraqi criminal courts. These courts are limited in number and may not be able to cope with all of the potential cases, without taking an unreasonably long time to resolve. Such delays may be a disservice to justice. That is why additional criminal courts will need to be set up in the respective Appellate Court districts, even if they are provisional and last only until the major caseload is handled.

A flow chart is attached which depicts a sample organization for these courts and commissions. (See Appendix A1/12)

e. Defenses: The Problem of Immunity Against Prosecution

Under Iraqi law, immunity does not pardon or annul a crime. It merely suspends legal proceedings for specific and special reasons. Lifting this immunity implies that the special reason for the restriction is removed and things are back to normal. In other words, the person enjoying immunity shall be subject to legal proceedings like any other person.

The 1970 interim constitution grants this immunity to the president, RCC members, ministers and Ba'ath party regional leadership members. Abolishing this constitution by the competent authority after regime change will automatically lift this immunity and restore normality. The question of military immunity is addressed in the section on institutional reform, where it is proposed that immunity for members of the military be lifted and that they be treated as civilians.

f. Amnesty

There are two kinds of amnesty. There is a general amnesty covering all perpetrators of crimes irrespective of their gravity and the persons involved. Such an amnesty has been applied in certain countries like Sierra Leone in 1999 and before it Argentina in 1983. It was unsuccessful as it had failed to restrain people's vengeful impulses and bring about the desired sense of justice. A general amnesty will not contribute to reconciliation in Iraq where the situation is much more complex. Objective conditions rule out this kind of amnesty in favour of other more relevant world experiences.

The amnesty deemed suitable for Iraq would be a qualified amnesty covering only specified abuses. It has been suggested that it should cover lesser offenses and infractions specified in the Iraqi criminal law. In other words, amnesty should be extended to crimes punishable by a maximum of five-year imprisonment. Other crimes, including criminal acts with international implications, should not be covered by the envisaged amnesty unless all of the victims or the victims' relatives settle for reconciliation, restitution according to local customs, or compensation for damages.

For the amnesty law to serve the purpose of reconciliation it should be contingent upon:

1. The persons amnestied turning themselves in within a specified time period.
2. The persons amnestied cooperating with the truth committees and fully and completely confessing their crimes.
3. The persons amnestied giving a public apology to the victims and the community as a whole.
4. The persons amnestied pledging not to repeat their misdeeds in the future.

This kind of amnesty has proved to be a success in South Africa. The essence of the amnesty is to acknowledge responsibility for previous abuses and cooperate with the truth committee investigators. On the basis of the findings, the committee will decide whether the perpetrator will be amnestied or not for reasons to be recorded in the investigation file.

2. Victim's Compensation and Reparations

Compensation to the victims of the Ba'ath regime since 1968 is a major component of the reconciliation process. It will soothe the victims' sense of having been unjustly treated and restrain their vengeful impulses while promoting trust between them and the new administration.

The regime's victims include those who lost loved ones in its prisons, were arbitrarily detained and tortured, lost their jobs, were expelled or forced into exile, had their property confiscated, were physically or psychologically scarred or have suffered significant injury; all deserve to be compensated for damages. (See Appendix B/21 for Draft Law enabling victim's compensation)

The two main kinds of compensation are:

1. Monetary compensation which may take two forms:

   a. Monetary compensation for confiscated real or personal property as a consequence of displacement, exile or unjust decrees.

   b. Monetary compensation for damages sustained as a consequence of the regime's actions, including persecution, murder, torture, imprisonment and detention on false charges.

2. Non-tangible compensation which may also be of two types:

   a. A formal apology to the victim or their relatives by the perpetrators if their abuses are covered by the amnesty or if the victim or their relatives accept such a gesture.

   b. A public registry listing of the victims to remind future generations of the regime's crimes and observing a certain day to commemorate the victims.

3. Recovery of Misappropriated Public Funds

The former regime consistently dispersed and dissipated public funds and deposited them in accounts and entities belonging to persons and private companies in order to conduct illegal businesses which serve the illegitimate purposes of this regime, unconcerned about the fate of this money so long as the persons in possession of these funds and property obey the orders of the regime.

As public funds are part and parcel of a nation's wealth and therefore all means and international contacts should be made to recover it, specific laws are recommended to criminalize the acts of persons in possession of this money and those who have failed to return it in the legally specified time to do so.

The laws call for all those in possession of misappropriated public funds/assets to return those funds/assets within 3 months from the issuance of this law. It is proposed that those who do return the funds/assets within this timeframe will be entitled to a 10% reward (of the value of the property). Those who do not return the property within this timeframe will be subject to prosecution. (See Appendix C/22 for Draft Law)

In addition, it is recommended that a commission be established to research and identify all companies who profited from doing business with the prior regime. This list should be published, and it would be up to the Iraqi electorate to determine what to do with these companies: whether to prosecute, blacklist, disgorge their ill-gotten profits or any other measures deemed appropriate. For the sake of posterity, it should be well known which businesses profited from their association with the prior regime.

4. De-Ba'athification

a. Revocation of Ba'ath Party Privileges

Since it seized power in 1968, the Baghdad regime has been granting privileges and lavish perks to members of the Ba'ath party from the public treasury without regard to the public's welfare. These privileges have been granted under laws passed by the regime, as handouts from Saddam Hussein himself or by arbitrary expropriation of public as well as personal funds and property.

There are ample examples of these excesses such as the confiscation of property belonging to deported or exiled individuals, distribution of housing plots, large financial rewards, houses, luxury cars, and other special prerogatives.

A draft law was drafted abolishing these privileges. (See Appendix D/31)

b. Memorialize Dark Ba'ath Era for Future Generations

The legacy of Saddam and his regime must not be lost on future generations of Iraqis. It is proposed that a monument for the regime's victims be built in every Iraqi city with a national museum of the regime's inhumane practices with a chronicle of the brutal methods used by its security agencies. Notorious prisons and torture chambers should be preserved as perpetual memorials for the victims of Saddam's crimes.

B. BUILDING THE FUTURE

1. Legal Reform

Laws affecting human rights and freedoms have been turned upside down and radically amended to assist the regime's violation of these very rights. It is, therefore, imperative to review major laws with the aim of restoring people's rights and dignity, including their right to a decent, secure life in their own country. Iraqi jurists in conjunction with international legal and human rights experts, have embarked on this project and make the following recommendations:

a. Criminal Law

The objective of criminal legislation is to maintain social order and protect public safety consistently and uniformly. By contrast, the Iraqi regime introduced amendments to the Iraqi penal code No 111 of 1969 in a manner contrary to human rights in order to secure its own survival.

In both its legislation and its actions the Iraqi regime has violated (and continues to violate) every aspect of humanitarian law as set forth in international covenants and the Universal Declaration of Human Rights. This includes imposing or increasing sentences with the death penalty without regard to the well-established legal principles that:

There is no crime and therefore no punishment without a specific text in the penal code.

Criminal laws cannot be retroactively applied.

The accused is innocent until proven guilty.

Sentencing decisions should be made specific to the individual defendant.

There should be no more than one punishment for the same crime.

The regime has also violated the basic rights of the accused, including the ban on torture and arbitrary detention, the right to compensation for damages, and freedom of speech.

The general consensus of the commentators is that the original Iraqi penal code and Criminal Procedure Code were drafted by a distinguished group of jurists, legal experts and judges. However, successive amendments were introduced by Saddam's regime which violate basic human rights and social norms. The main purpose for these amendments was to ensure the survival of the regime.

Nonetheless, the entire criminal code needs to be overhauled under a legitimate process that is in keeping with the times and technological advances. However, this process should be the result of a thorough study and examination by legal experts who should undertake this task in a stable environment with a functioning parliament (legislative body) under favourable conditions for enacting a modern criminal code.

In the meantime, the offensive amendments which violate basic human rights should be dealt with in the interim period. The majority of the commentators are in favour of keeping the existing penal code and Criminal Procedure Code after repealing all amendments and modifications by the authority empowered to enact laws during the transitional period.

Specifically, it is proposed to repeal all provisions regarding political offences in articles 20, 21 and 22 of the penal code.

It is also proposed to amend the Criminal Procedure Code to give defense lawyers the absolute right to be present and to see all papers related to the case at every phase, and to visit their clients in custody without interference by any state authority.

In culmination, a bill has been drafted repealing all amendments in question. (See Appendix E/28)

b. Military Penal Codes

Military penal codes are marked by two main characteristics:

1. Immunity and extensive powers.

   Law No 106 of 1960 on Service of Process has turned members of the military into a privileged class. It grants them immunity against summons and legal proceedings by civil courts. Indeed, it almost absolves them of all liability. A member of the military can be apprehended only when committing a witnessed crime. Even in this case the accused shall be handed over to the nearest military authority. The accused can be brought before a civil court only with approval of the minister of defense or an official authorized by him. Also, military courts have extensive jurisdiction. (See Appendix F/8)

2. Severity of punishment.

   The military penal code is also marked by its harsh penalties in matters related to security of the regime or its military and repressive agencies. Military courts have been granted extensive powers although their member judges generally lack the necessary legal qualifications to decide cases referred to their courts.

   The military penal code provides for severe penalties that are out of tune with modern criminal practice. Iraqi military penal codes are a fairly realistic reflection of the "carrot and stick" policy pursued by the regime. Members of the military enjoy extensive privileges and immunity against prosecution for crimes committed against civilians. On the other hand, they are subject to extremely harsh penalties for offences related to security of the regime and its military institutions.

Recommendation

1. The jurisdiction of military courts is dealt with under Institutional Reform-Judiciary.
2. With regard to immunity, there is no justification whatsoever for members of the military to be more privileged than others or be elevated to a distinct class from the rest of the people. This immunity must be revoked.

c. Nationality law

Since the coup of 8 February 1963, Iraqi citizenship matters are governed by law No. 43 of 1963 repealing law No. 42 of 1924 and its amendments.

The general consensus is that the existing law has introduced unjust provisions that have resulted in the tragic deportation of tens of thousands of Iraqis after revoking their citizenship. That is why this law constitutes a flagrant violation of human rights pursuant to international covenants and the Universal Declaration of Human Rights. Article 15 of the latter states that every individual has the right to citizenship. It also states that a person cannot be arbitrarily denied citizenship or the right to change it.

It is agreed that this law and its amendments cannot remain effective after a regime change as hundreds of thousands have been victimized by it. It should be repealed in its entirety while recognizing the naturalization decisions taken under it.

A review should be undertaken to compensate victims and restore Iraqi citizenship to those who have unjustly lost it. There should also be a watchdog entity established to oversee implementation of the new law with a view to guaranteeing people's rights.

Work in this connection has culminated in drafting a new citizenship law taking into account the problems caused by previous laws as much as possible until a new, well-considered citizenship law is adopted by the prospective Iraqi parliament. It should be noted that, unlike most other nationality laws in the region, this proposed law is gender neutral. (See Appendix G/29)

d. Administrative law

The Baghdad regime's policy since it seized power has resulted in rife corruption in the state apparatus. The main causes for the corrupt bureaucracy may be summed up in the following:

1. Politicization of administration.
2. The economic squeeze and low wages.
3. Absence of administrative, legal, parliamentary and public controls over the bureaucracy.
4. Militarization of the administration.

Recommendation

To uplift the state bureaucracy to the level of democratic transformation in Iraq during the transition period, a host of reforms must be carried out, including:

Repealing all laws and decrees that have politicized administrative functions and terminating control of state institutions by the ruling party;

Reviewing civil service and employment laws with incentives encouraging honesty and integrity with an emphasis on the concept of the "public trust" for civil servants;

Establishing administrative, judicial, public and parliamentary oversight over civil servants;

Preparing a development plan for the administration of the bureaucracy;

Identifying and dismissing all employees found to be redundant, corrupt, or grossly negligent in their duties;

Selecting top civil servants who are highly qualified people of unquestionable integrity to set an example for their staff; and

Developing intensive plans to train civil servants at various levels such as:

Introducing modern technology in administrative work.

Promoting courteous interaction at all levels of the system and renouncing condescending attitudes within the system or towards the public.

Disbanding all state functions or positions related to the Ba'ath party—including those of security officers and operations run by that party in the state bureaucracy.

Reviewing all other laws governing the bureaucratic function for further reform in line with the new democratic era.

Considering the crucial nature of the transitional phase and the fact that the Ba'ath party is primarily responsible for politicizing and therefore crippling the bureaucracy, a bill has been drafted repealing the "leading party law" No. 142 of 1974 and banning the Ba'ath party itself. (See Appendix H/30)

e. Civil Law

The general consensus of the commentators is that the existing civil law of 1951 has not experienced any radical change in contravention of human rights. Maintaining this law will not be detrimental to these rights, at least and until specialized legal authorities are in place to re-examine the law and present relevant recommendations.

f. Interim laws

These are laws expected to be required during the transitional period to deal with immediate situations and needs. A body of legal experts should be set up to examine these needs, which may be called "Ad hoc Legal Committee for Drafting Interim Laws." The Judicial Council may assist with this task during the transitional period.

Immediately after a regime change, it will be imperative to pass a law banning the Ba'ath party and privileges enjoyed by it under the "leading party law" No. 142 of 1974 as it was used as a tool of persecution and brutal repression.

2. Institutional Reform

The vital state institutions have undergone extensive changes in their structure and functions dissociating them from the purposes they were originally set up to serve. Their function changed from serving and protecting the public to solely serving and protecting Saddam and his regime.

This is why it is a critical manifestation of transitional justice to reform these institutions and re-establish their basic public services. Reform cannot be brought about by merely renaming the institutions that supported the dictatorship. Reform demands restructuring of these institutions and the laws under which they operate to serve the public good rather than the repressive regime. The most important institutions are the judiciary, institute of legal education, security agencies, military and prison system to name but a few.

a. Judiciary

Before the coup of 17 July 1968, the Iraqi judiciary was marked by a measure of integrity, impartiality and commitment to the requirements of justice. It enjoyed a certain degree of independence in fulfilling its duties and making its rulings, which were characterized by the principle of even-handedness, solid substantiation and profound legal reasoning. These rulings would serve as precedents to be cited by litigants and other courts alike.

Before the 1968 coup, the Iraqi judiciary ensured a modest level of justice in the sphere of social order and individual rights. This was the result of concerns by successive governments to uphold the integrity of this vital sphere. There is no denying, however, that all those governments were undemocratic and opposed to judicial scrutiny of their political actions, including the legislative process and the actions of the executive.

After the 1968 coup the Ba'ath regime introduced the notion that there are no independent state powers except one political power assisted by legislative, executive and judicial agencies to undertake its responsibilities. This eliminated any notion of the separation of powers (legislative, executive and judiciary) and turned all of these powers into institutions controlled by one ultimate political power under Saddam Hussein.

To eliminate any remaining role for an independent judiciary, the Baghdad regime dissolved the Judicial Council which was headed by the presiding judge of the Iraqi cassation court. It was re-invented as "the justice council" headed by the minister of justice who reported to the President.

As a consequence, the Iraqi judge has become a mere functionary following orders from the political power. The breakdown below demonstrates the unparalleled fragmented nature of the current Iraqi judiciary:

The Iraqi judiciary is divided into the following sectors:

i. The Iraq cassation court.

ii. The military cassation court.

iii. The internal security agencies cassation court.

iv. Special judiciary courts, which are divided into four parts:

1. The revolutionary court.

2. Judiciary of party organizations. (Serious judicial powers have been granted to party organizations.)

3. Judiciary of ministries and security agencies. (Many courts have been set up in key ministries and departments like the interior, defense and security agencies—intelligence, public security and special security).

4. Judiciary of provisional courts.

v. Judiciary of the joint cassation court.

vi. Judiciary of special powers. (Judicial powers granted to state functionaries, police officers and others.)

Each of the above judicial organs is completely separate from the other, and they are in no way connected with each other. Each of them is linked to a specific ministry or government agency. Each has its own functions defined by its own laws.

Recommendations

Justice and human rights have been the first victims of this decimation of the Iraqi judiciary. The transitional authority will have the urgent task of restoring the authority of the Iraqi judiciary and its former uniform structure as much as possible pending a more detailed plan to ensure the independence of this branch and its jurisdiction over all aspects of the legal system in Iraq. To this end the following steps are proposed after a regime change:

1. Abolishing all special courts and powers granted to police, security and intelligence officers as well as other state functionaries. (See Appendix I/49 for Draft Law)
2. Keeping for the time being military courts and internal security courts governed by law No 44 of 1941 on military court procedures. These courts will be difficult to dissolve due to the service laws involved and it will take some time to review these laws together with the penal codes. However, the jurisdiction of these courts can be restricted to only enforcing the military penal code. Civilian criminal courts shall have jurisdiction over all other crimes subject to the provisions of any other penal code like crimes committed by a member of the military against another or against a civilian.
3. Incorporating all lower cassation courts into the Iraq cassation court. A body should be created within its structure to try crimes covered by the military penal code. This body may co-opt an expert on the military penal code such as the head of the legal department at the ministry of defense, his counterpart at the ministry of interior, a legal officer with a minimum of ten-years of experience or any other officer whose participation is deemed necessary for technical reasons.
4. Setting up a higher constitutional court to serve as a watchdog over the constitutionality of laws, by-laws and decrees and their accord with the provisions of the constitution and international covenants of human rights, including the Universal Declaration of Human Rights.
5. Setting up a judiciary council comprised of the presiding judge of the Iraq cassation court, his deputies, presiding judges of the lower cassation courts, presiding judges of the appeal courts, presiding judge of the higher constitutional court, his deputies, president of the state consultative council, his deputies, chief of the prosecutor's office and head of the justice department's inspectorate.
6. Amending the law No. 160 of 1979 on organizing the judiciary in line with the transitional justice project while ensuring total independence of the judiciary. (See Appendix J/50 for Draft law)

b. Internal and Other Security Agencies

The Baghdad regime relies on special security agencies it created which have no relationship to the conventional internal security agencies operating in the Iraqi state when it was founded. These special security agencies are: the general intelligence (mukhabarat), special security, Fyda'een Saddam, the special republican guard, the people's army, the emergency forces and the Al-Quds Army.

All of them are repressive agencies that have extensive powers and their own prisons and detention centers. They used torture and extrajudicial killing to terrorize the people.

The regular internal security agencies consist of the police general directorate, the security general directorate, the traffic police general directorate, the citizenship general directorate and the border police general directorate.

These agencies have been in existence since before the British occupation in 1918. After the occupation, the commander of British forces issued a police statement No. 72 of 1920 setting out guidelines governing police affairs. The internal security agencies developed further, and police service and discipline law No 20 of 1943 was later enacted to regulate their function. This law was more akin to the civil service law than to the military service law; in fact, the civil service law was its main source.

The internal security agencies have been militarized under the Ba'ath regime and subjected to service laws similar to those of military service and military penal codes. They have been granted extraordinary immunity as is the case with military personnel.

Recommendations

Recommendations with regard to all of the "special" security agencies are strongly in favour of disbanding them and liquidating their assets immediately after a regime change as they will be superfluous and irrelevant.

A draft resolution has been drawn up disbanding the special security agencies. (See Appendix K/37)

To reform the relationship of the regular security agencies with the public, it is proposed that a new motto be established: "police in the service of the people." These institutions should be re-built to focus solely on the protection of social order, individual rights and public safety. The laws governing these agencies should be reviewed and transformed into civil laws.

The training and education of their personnel needs to be redesigned to ensure they serve the purpose which they were originally designed to serve. To ensure the people's freedoms and rights it is equally necessary to abolish the immunity enjoyed by these agencies under the Service of Process law No. 106 of 1960.

c. Military Service (The draft)

The Iraqi people, especially young Iraqis, have suffered tragically as a result of the Baghdad regime's misadventures and wars with neighbouring countries. Hundreds of thousands of young Iraqis have been killed or disabled due to continued compulsory service in the army which has consumed the better part of life for this age group.

An international protection force under the auspices of the United Nations, after regime change, will allow Iraqis to use their creative potential for building a new Iraq, especially the young people. The new Iraq must be at peace with itself, its neighbours and the world refraining from destabilizing the region while focusing on democracy building. This requires the rejection of any thinking to build a new war machine as it will be meaningless and incompatible with the aspirations of a new democratic Iraq seeking peace and goodwill.

Accordingly, the commentators see no need for compulsory military service. Instead there should be a professional army of volunteers to defend the country against external aggression. A new Iraq belonging to the community of democratic states can contribute to international efforts to establish the principles of justice and to fight international terrorism.

d. Prison System

Prison law No. 51 of 1969 was apparently passed within the framework of a reasonable penal policy to turn the prison system into an agency for reform and rehabilitation of its inmates. However, the regime's practices, its manner of operating the prisons, and the punishments meted out by the regime run counter to the aims of the above law. Punishment under Saddam's regime serves as revenge rather than reform. Amendments to the Iraqi penal code abound with prescriptions for capital punishment for minor offences, albeit primarily political offences. Indeed, the regime has introduced such inhumane punishment as chopping off ears, branding, amputation of the limbs and other prehistoric forms of punishment that are diametrically opposed to modern penal policy. Inhumane treatment is widespread against prisoners and detainees.

Recommendation

The following negative aspects of the prison law need to be eliminated:

1. Solitary confinement as a punitive measure during which the prisoner is denied regular meals.
2. Section 7 of the prison law dealing with political prisoners and detainees, which grossly contradicts democratic practice under the prospective new government. Self-expression and opposition are by no means a crime punishable by law, and, therefore, there should be no political prisoners. This section must be repealed.

It is proposed to add the following new provisions:

1. None of the punitive measures laid down in the prison law may be enforced without an inquiry. In the course of such inquiry the prisoner is faced with the alleged offence and given a hearing with the right to self-defense. There should be a written record of the proceeding.
2. None of these punitive measures should entail delay of release after serving the sentence passed or the order of remand.
3. Defense lawyers shall have the right to meet privately with the detained or imprisoned defendant. Foreign detainees or prisoners shall have access to

their respective consulates or the mission representing their country's interests.

4. No staff members of a public authority may contact any detainee or prisoner without a written consent from the general prosecutor.
5. Any pregnant woman prisoner shall be accorded special treatment and medical care from the date pregnancy has become evident.
6. Special treatment shall be accorded the mentally ill prisoner. Upon determination of the prisoner's condition, he/she shall be moved to a mental institution.
7. Release may be obtained for health reasons if it is established that a prisoner has a life-threatening condition or the prisoner's condition poses a threat to the lives of others in prison. Release for health reasons shall be effected by a decision of the general prosecutor with a copy of the decision to the ministry of labour and social affairs.
8. Prisoner's relatives shall be informed if his/her condition has become sufficiently serious.
9. Bodies of dead prisoners shall be turned over to their relatives with a detailed report on the history of illness, the nature of work on the day of death, the kind of food, the date the prisoner was committed to hospital, the date when the condition was first diagnosed, the specific nature of illness, the last day a doctor examined the prisoner and the date and time of death.

For a Draft law implementing these recommendation see Appendix L/54.

e. Institute for Legal Reform and Training of Lawyers

There is at present a judicial institute affiliated with the ministry of justice. It has two-year courses to graduate judges and general practice attorneys. This institute can be developed to offer three-year courses, including one or two years for practical training in the work of judges and public prosecutors. Also, its curriculum should be re-examined to be consistent with Iraq's future development.

Courses at the institute can be expanded to the training of lawyers and legal personnel. As the institute is engaged in the training of judicial personnel in general, a body specialized in legal reform at the institute will be very relevant. Reform questions can be discussed with competent legal personnel at the institute.

3. Proposed Constitutional Principles

Having universally accepted constitutional principles is important at any stage of governance in Iraq. No state function can be fulfilled by the various authorities without a constitution as the basic law. Serious thought must given to the issue of constitutional principles during the transitional period. Without these supreme rules ensuring people's rights and defining their duties, transitional justice in Iraq will be unthinkable.

Iraq's multi-ethnic, multi-religious and multi-cultural structure has been further compounded by Saddam's sectarian policy. Working out constitutional principles for such a country will be a daunting task. A permanent constitution at this or any subsequent stage can only deliberated with the full involvement of the public as well as all political groups and personalities in post-Saddam Iraq.

The transitional stage will be better served with transitional constitutional principles that will serve as a basis for the authority of state powers and a guarantee of people's rights. Such principles should be drafted by a team of experts—technocrats—specialized in law, political science, sociology and economics.

Recommendation

It is proposed that the future transitional constitution or basic law include the following principles:

1. Separation of the three branches (legislative, executive and judicial) and defining the character of each branch, its structure, duties and mechanism of discharging its functions.
2. Recognition of Iraq's multi-ethnic structure comprising Arabs, Kurds, Turkmans and Assyrians among other ethnic groups.
3. Recognition that Iraq is a multi-religious society, including Islam, Christianity, Judaism, Mandaeim, Yazidism, and religious communities like the Shiites, Sunnis, etc.
4. Commitment to international covenants ensuring human rights in Iraq, including the Universal Declaration of Human Rights.

5. Upholding people's basic rights and responsibilities, including safeguarding property and banning unlawful confiscation.

    Equality in rights and duties and prohibition against all forms of discrimination.

    The principle that the accused is innocent until proven guilty.

    The principle of non-retroactivity of criminal and economic laws.

    Non-interference in people's private affairs like the freedom of thought, faith, etc.

    Prohibition of torture.

    Commitment to other related humanitarian principles.

6. Recognition of cultural rights and languages of all nationalities.
7. Freedom of worship rites and religious freedom for all communities.
8. Right of regular courts to oversee constitutionality of laws or assigning this task to a constitutional court.
9. Maintaining the present administrative provincial divisions until a permanent constitution is adopted, and state constitutional structures are in place in the course of democratic transformation.
10. Any other basic principles that contribute to stability without controversy with groups inside Iraq.

It should be pointed out that any attempt to enforce any of Iraq's past constitutions since 1925 will antagonize one group or another in Iraq and provoke senseless disputes. The republicans refuse to recognize the 1925 constitution; the monarchists refuse the republican constitutions; and the Kurds do not recognize any constitution that does not guarantee their right to federalism.

It will, therefore, be more practical to adopt a transitional constitution drafted by competent experts. Such a constitution should ensure the separation of the branches and protect human rights and the basic norms of citizenship.

4. Recommendations for Authority in Transitional Phase

It should be emphasized that the basic principle for a transitional authority in Iraq is that it should be comprised of Iraqis. The qualifications should be established such that any person serving on a transitional authority should have:

1. A solid track record of service to the country;
2. Sound moral character and unquestioned integrity;
3. No prior associations with Saddam's regime which might taint his/her reputation; and
4. No prior involvement or even appearance of involvement with criminal activities or other improprieties.

Furthermore, it is recommended that anyone with executive authority in the transitional phase be ineligible for participating in the first round of elections. Since one of the tasks of the transitional authority will be to prepare for the first round of elections, it is imperative there not be any conflict of interest issues.

In addition, the affairs of the state should be run by technical experts (i.e., technocrats) in key areas. It is proposed that the branches at this stage are as follows:

1. *The Executive:* Consisting of, first, a presidential council which is proposed to be comprised of 3–5 Iraqi members representing Iraq's diversified structure. Needless to say, members of the presidential council must be people known for their independent thinking, integrity, expertise and good reputation in Iraqi society; and, second, a council of ministers: comprising highly experienced Iraqi technocrats known for their independent thinking and good reputation in Iraqi society.

2. *The Judiciary:* Represented by a judicial council of high-level judges. The council may be headed by the presiding judge of the Iraq cassation court. Its membership may consist of the presiding judge of the cassation court, of course, his deputies, presiding judges of civil, family, administrative and criminal courts, presiding judge of the higher constitutional court, his deputies, president of the state consultative council, his deputies, head of the judicial inspectorate, head of the law drafting department and presiding judges of appeal courts. The judicial council may be authorized to decide on all matters related to judges like appointment, promotion, allowances, retirement, etc. The presiding judge and members of the judicial council are to have the same grade and privileges as the president and members of the council of ministers. The council is to have

its own budget separate from that of the justice ministry to ensure maximum independence of the judiciary in the interests of justice and democracy in post-Saddam Iraq. An independent judiciary is a solid guarantee for the establishment of the rule of law.

3. *The Legislative:* The transitional period will be without a parliament to pass laws. A safe arrangement on the path to a democratic and just society is for both the executive and the judiciary to jointly pass laws. Legislation at this stage should not be left to the executive alone lest it establish a monopoly in this sphere. In other words, the legislative during the transitional period will be a combination of the presidential council, the council of ministers and the judicial council pending the formal approval of a permanent constitution and development of constitutional institutions.

Possible Violence and Resistance to Change

Since it seized power in 1968 the Baghdad regime has surrounded itself with different centers designed to tighten its grip on the internal situation. These centers are a major part of an array of potential factors that may trigger acts of violence and resistance to the expected change in Iraq.

To preempt such potential risks these factors have to be identified keeping in mind the situation cannot be totally controlled due to the political minefields created by the Saddam regime. Effective action is still required to minimize any losses that may be sustained as a consequence.

The main risk factors and how to deal with them:

A. *Sectarianism.* Saddam Hussein has used every possible means to ensure his survival in power. This has taken a heavy human and material toll affecting all components of Iraqi society. Saddam Hussein has always been aware how unpopular he is. To find support in the region and within Iraq he has played the sectarian card in his policies and official propaganda. He has been suggesting to Sunni army officers that they are the first to be targeted in the coming change and that is why they have to remain on his side for their own survival. His media has been working 'round the clock to fuel sectarian discord with a view to winning supporters at home and in the region.

Saddam's ploys to use the sectarian card for winning support at home and in the region must be effectively countered by a plan focused on exposing the dangers of sectarianism.

B. *Involvement in Saddam's Crimes.* To tie the fate of as many state officials as possible to his own, Saddam has involved them in his crimes as members of the Revolutionary Command Council, ministers, security officials, military commanders or party commissars.

People involved in lesser abuses than war crimes, crimes against humanity, torture or genocide under international criminal law, should be given hope that they may be amnestied in a general pardon and national reconciliation process. It will be also useful to cite article 129 of law No 23 of 1971 on Criminal Procedure Code concerning the possibility of appeal bargains and amnesty to those who admit to their abuses and provide information about other suspects in the interests of a proper investigation. Such steps will give those people hope and encourage them to defect.

C. *Economic Benefits and Bribery.* During his years in power Saddam has created an army of beneficiaries, whether by perks or privileges to officers serving in the republican guard and special republican guard and other personnel in the security agencies, his body guards, etc. Others are bought off by cash rewards distributed every now and then. Contractors are bribed by lucrative deals. Even dissidents and expatriates have been stigmatized with salaries, allowances and grants to start up businesses. Others have been hired as consultants to government oil companies.

The discourse to be adopted in this regard should be reassuring to those who have legitimately benefited from doing business with the regime, who have received payments for certain normal services and those who have won contracts in clean bidding.

D. *New Class.* Saddam has created a new class of tribal chiefs who have been given money, arms and limousines in return for controlling their tribesmen.

Those tribal leaders can be won over through contacts they still have with Iraqi exiles or by a clear message that they can keep their privileges so long as they side with the people against dictatorship.

E. *Score Settling and Vengeful Acts.* Saddam Hussein and his cohorts are guilty of war crimes, genocide, crimes against humanity, extrajudicial killings, plunder, rape, torture, displacement and unlawful expropriation of property. These atrocities have created entire groups of victims impatient for revenge and score-settling when the opportunity presents itself after a regime change with a possible breakdown of security structures. That is what happened during the March 1991 uprising. Actions by victims or their relatives are bound to be accompanied by common criminal acts. After all, crime is a phenomenon seen in all societies with various degrees depending on economic, political, psychological, social and genetic factors. Iraqi society is no different. It has its own criminals who are a product of these conditions. Saddam's regime has further aggravated these factors by its inhumane policies in all spheres. Indeed, it has released all common criminals some of whom are likely to revert to their old habits. The period immediately after regime change might offer these criminals an opportunity to engage in acts of killing, plunder, looting, etc.

To foil people seeking revenge and the potential acts of common criminals, it is necessary to take a host of decisive measures, including:

1. Impose a 24-hour curfew on the first day to be gradually relaxed according to the extent of security and order established.
2. Order all police forces to be on their guard and arrest all offenders.
3. Organize military patrols by coalition forces in all major cities to prevent lawlessness, especially against vital utilities and key government facilities.
4. Instruct tribal and clan leaders to use their authority to control rural areas.
5. Propagate the new laws and decrees via all mass media, including the use of airplanes. A stern warning is to be issued against any revenge acts targeting government officials as a crime punishable by law. It should be made clear that law, order and justice are a prime concern and that all criminals against the people will be brought to trials.
6. Give explicit orders to the border guard and army units stationed on the border to tighten their control and block all escape routes that may be used by wanted criminals or for intervention by other forces to cause disturbances in Iraq.
7. Make appeals to all hospital, ambulance, civil defense, water, electricity and other utility personnel to immediately report to duty.
8. Make appeals to all government employees and the public as a whole to maintain law and order and protect state property, including museums, public buildings and other facilities against any acts of sabotage or vandalism.
9. Assemble investigation teams, truth and reconciliation committees and criminal courts without delay in order to reassure the people that the new administration will safeguard their rights.

5. Public Education and Awareness of Human/Civil Rights

Legal awareness is lacking even among Iraqi intellectuals. The reason is indifference by Iraqi society and disinterest by the state towards laws as they have both been in the grip of despotism.

Awareness of laws and rights will help people shed the despotic, dictatorial thinking in favour of tolerance, understanding the need for public participation in governance as well as the peaceful transition from one administration to another in government. People with good legal understanding of their rights will be in a better position to identify danger signs which run counter to the rule of law and democratic practice. Law, after all, is the outcome of such practice when it is enacted by democratically elected legislatures.

How can public awareness of their rights be promoted? It can only be fostered by harnessing all required resources in society towards this end. We have to start with the education system and the media as well as laws that will give people a sense of security and ensure justice for them. For this awareness to be in step with the new reality, the laws that are passed must meet people's actual needs.

Considering the appalling state of culture and media in Iraq due to the regime's policy, a forward-looking vision has to be developed for Iraqi culture and media in terms of public awareness and methodology. The Saddam regime has politicized culture and turned the media into a propaganda machine serving its own purposes. That is why it is imperative for the future Iraqi media to be independent and unfettered promoting freedom of expression and transparency. The media will act as a vox populi reflector and a watchdog over government actions and state institutions. Another prerequisite of media and cultural work is free access to information and educating the young Iraqi generation in a spirit of tolerance and multiculturalism.

That is why it is important to focus on promoting legal awareness as well in the curricula of journalism faculties and the media as a whole. Teaching legal subjects will contribute to a public culture that may serve as a mass education for democracy while excluding the culture of violence and personality cult. Saddam's regime has undermined rational, humanitarian education, misguided the young generation and trampled such values as fair play and equal opportunity. Attention should be paid to re-educate the young generation for its members to be good, well qualified and scientifically equipped citizens capable of safeguarding the people's democratic gains.

Iraq is the land of great civilizations that prospered in climates of inter-cultural coexistence. To revive such positive elements in our heritage, publications and mass communications should be free from all forms of censorship. The private sector should be enabled to compete with state-owned media, and this also goes for the arts in general as an essential component of national culture.

The rule of law will be jeopardized in the absence of legal awareness on the part of both government employees and the public. It will be absurd for state laws to remain the domain of scholars and experts. These laws should be part of the public domain for their enforcement to be meaningful. (See Appendix M/66 for Draft Law to Create Human Rights Organization in Iraq).

UNITED STATES INSTITUTE OF PEACE

CONCLUSIONS OF USIP ROUNDTABLE ON LESSONS LEARNED FROM PRIOR VETTING PROCESSES[1]

(January 24, 2003)

I. Why is vetting critical to the success of a democratic transition?

Vetting is necessary in order to:

1. Sanction those who have committed abuses and remove them from positions in which they could continue to do so.
2. Instill public confidence in the reformed and cleansed institutions of government. The vetting process can serve as a means of inculcating new social norms, promoting government legitimacy, and building a new sense of civic responsibility and national identity. This emphasis is increasingly preferred under international standards to the Point (1)'s focus on patently punitive vetting.
3. Render the handling of past abuse more manageable. Even if prosecutions occur for abuses of the ousted regime, there will be very few trials relative to the number of potential cases.
4. Contribute to public order. A hesitant, arbitrary or incomplete vetting process can likewise result in personal vengeance, festering grievances, and lack of public trust in government.

II. Who does the vetting?

Vetting may be conducted by (1) one centralized government agency or specially established commission; (2) separately by each ministry and agency; (3) by foreign occupation authorities; or (4) by an international interim authority; or (5) by a combination of the above. In the last two cases, it will be essential that carefully selected and publicly credible locals participate in or advise the process. If local authority is to have responsibility for the vetting process, international pressure can be important to ensure implementation and enforcement of vetting decisions.

Authority: In most cases, vetting is based on the enactment of a law, the imposition of a decree by governing authority, or the provision for vetting in a peace accord. Vetting will often be subject to charges of arbitrariness and "victor's justice," making it important to clarify the standards and procedures to be applied. A greater expectation applies in this regard in the vetting of the civilian sector than security forces. Whenever possible, make use of local laws and legal principles. This legitimates the process in the eyes of both accused and surrounding public.

III. Who gets vetted and when?

Vetting requires balancing the need to purge with the necessity of "keeping the trains running." The need to have sufficient personnel in place to run essential government functions, especially security functions, may constrain the thoroughness of an initial purge. Before beginning any purge, determine (a) the availability of qualified replacements; (b) the time it will take to recruit/train new personnel; and (c) the level of disruption that will ensue in any institution during a gap between dismissed and new personnel.

It is essential to determine—and prioritize—which positions in which sectors should be vetted lest they pose a threat to immediate post-conflict security and undermine public confidence in the transition. (In various cases, this has included the military, security, intelligence forces, judiciary, teachers, financial officials, media, and health professionals.)

In the initial phase, vetting must focus on removal of unsuitable personnel from police and security forces. This serves to enforce immediate public order for the interim administration, break up cabals of corrupt or criminal officers, and dissuade victims from taking private vengeance.

Vetting of prosecutorial and judicial personnel must keep pace with the vetting of security and police forces in order to ensure a functioning justice system. Leaving

[1] With the encouragement of senior NSC staff, the United States Institute of Peace organized a roundtable discussion on January 9th, 2003 involving former U.S. government officials and non-governmental experts on the experiences of several countries with efforts to screen and purge the security forces and civilian administration during a transition from a repressive system to democracy. Prior cases that were discussed included post-WWII Germany and France, the purge of the military in El Salvador, de-Stasification of various sectors following German re-unification, and police vetting programs in the Balkans, Haiti and elsewhere.

corrupt judges in place can undermine efforts to reform police forces and can facilitate a return to police abuse.

Vetting must take place in all areas of government, and often in the private sector as well as the public sector, in order for the public to feel justice has been served. Private sector vetting may follow its own procedures, but should be monitored so as not to violate the democratic principles that will govern under the new regime.

As seen in several prior cases, accusations and purges can easily get out of control. Vetting should be thorough, particularly in the security forces, police and judiciary, but should be constrained.

IV. What Criteria are applied?

In previous vetting programs in various countries, the following categories of implicated personnel have been excluded from key positions on the basis of vetting:

Senior officers (e.g. from colonels up), except as truly needed;

War criminals and human rights abusers;

Secret police informants;

Senior party officials;

Drug traffickers/members of criminal syndicates; and

Those deemed unqualified based on professional history and competence.

V. What sources of information provide the basis for vetting?

Ideally, vetting should be based on a comprehensive review of as many sources of information as possible given the possibility of incomplete, missing, and falsified records. It is necessary, therefore, to be able to fuse/filter disparate sources of information and to account for distorted/politically-based allegations.

It is imperative to immediately locate, secure and restrict access to all relevant personnel records, intelligence files, court and prison records, and other relevant databases as quickly as possible. These will provide the main basis for vetting. Unsecured, these records will be destroyed, falsified, or used for blackmail. In addition to records of the new deposed government, vetting can draw on data from publicly available news sources, international human rights groups, and foreign intelligence sources. Compile as many records and sources of information as possible before the transition.

Elements of vetting review:

1. Records and data sources as noted above.
2. Publication of candidate lists (ideally in local papers and in refugee centers abroad), with a request for the public to submit any relevant information regarding candidates.
3. Applicants should be required to self-report their history and activities, with any falsehood being an immediate disqualifier. Self-reported histories can be crosschecked against available records and witness testimony. Misrepresentations, even impersonations, are common.
4. Vetting review must not only clear an individual of culpability for abuses of the old regime, but also determine his/her objective qualifications and ability to adapt to the norms and practices of a new, accountable and civilian-led democratic government.

VI. What are the key procedural considerations?

Fewer cases versus faster processing: Vetting can target and purge specific individuals based on past abuses. This is by definition retrospective and retributive, and consequently a higher due process standard is required. Alternatively, all current holders of the designated positions are required to re-apply. In this case, vetting is prospective and, like routine civil service screening, a lower due process burden can be applied to the program. In the second scenario, continuation of the applicants in their jobs is contingent on eventual approval in the vetting process—making it possible to more quickly remove targeted individuals while review of other cases proceeds more slowly.

Due process: Three due process questions routinely arise: (1) Is there a right of the vettee to confront the evidence against him/her? (2) Is representation by counsel permitted? (3) Can vetting decisions be appealed? Provision for a limited appeals process is helpful, particularly for civilian positions, in that a successful appeal by an accused abuser vindicates the legitimacy of the vetting process.

Standardization: Vetting rules may (1) be rigid and uniform, to expedite the process and avoid the appearance or reality of arbitrariness, or (2) allow for subjective evaluation, taking into account such factors as severity of misdeeds, mitigating factors, coercion or other reasons for taking the action in question, later remorse/ change in conduct, or distance in time from the abuse.

Duration: Dismissal from the security forces may be permanent, given concern over renewed abuses. Civilian vetting, on the other hand, is usually of temporary duration (typically 5–10 years) to allow breathing space for government and society to re-create itself, after which they move to a level playing field.

VII. What happens to the purged?

Types of sanctions which may result from vetting: Those sanctions which have been employed in various countries include employment dismissal; exclusion from appointed office; exclusion from elected office; exclusion from designated private sector positions or professions; denial of benefits (including government pension); exclusion from suffrage.

Prevent the purged from becoming spoilers: Those vetted out cannot simply be sent home, but must be placed in some sort of organized, remunerated activity. This temporarily ensures their livelihood so they do not turn to criminal activity, facilitates observation of their interactions with former colleagues, and prevents them from organizing a troublemaking underground force.

VIII. What happens to those who survive the vetting process?

Probation: Those retained—particularly in the police and security forces—should be retained on a probationary basis. The probationary period should be long enough to (1) allow refugees to return and provide additional relevant information, and (2) permit monitoring of performance to ensure suitability. This may last up to two years. It may be useful to put outside personnel in place to closely supervise the work of these remaining employees during this period.

UNITED STATES INSTITUTE OF PEACE

Project on Constitution-Making, Peace Building, and National Reconciliation

Since the age of Enlightenment and the revolutions in France and the United States, constitutionalism has played an ever-increasing role in nation-building and in the establishment of the rule of law. At the dawn of the twenty-first century, nations of virtually every region of the world recognize the role of constitutionalism in their own political and legal systems. The recent and dramatic increase in the number of new and transitional nations adopting democratic constitutions attests to the significance of constitution-making to democracy, national reconciliation, and political development. In many countries making the transition from civil war, one of the first tasks undertaken is the drafting of a new constitution. Insofar as the constitution articulates the vision of a new society, defines the fundamental principles by which the country will be reorganized, and redistributes power within the country, it can play an important role in the consolidation of peace.

A variety of projects and publications have focused on the substance of constitutions in response to conflict, often highlighting the role of such concepts as federalism or separation of powers. Surprisingly little work has been done, however, to examine the extent to which the process of creating a constitution can become a vehicle for national dialogue and the consolidation of peace, allowing competing perspectives and claims within the post-war society to be aired and incorporated. This is the focus of the *Project on Constitution-Making, Peace Building, and National Reconciliation,* co-sponsored by the United States Institute of Peace and the United Nations Development Program.

Many issues to be confronted in the crafting of a post-conflict constitution can accentuate fundamental differences and lead to renewed factionalization. Choices made as to the timing of the process could be perceived as favoring one group over another. The role and organization of political parties in the constitution-making process may reopen old wounds or recall ethnic or other rivalries. The choice of electoral systems for a constitutional convention could have similar effects. The subject of human rights, and the question of participation in the constitution-making process of those who recently perpetrated major abuses, may be so volatile as to incite renewed accusations and conflict. The project is also considering certain substantive issues that, while outside the project's primary scope, are potentially divisive and impact on questions of process. On the other hand, the constitution-making process can be a potent element in the reduction of conflict. The more that the constitution-making process develops a sense of confidence in parties to the conflict and in the public in general that the new constitutional framework will protect their interests and will provide them with non-violent avenues for defending their rights, for example, the more it will contribute to the building of a stable peace. The project seeks to develop guidelines for strengthening such positive dynamics in the post-conflict context.

The project's inter-disciplinary Working Group is chaired by Professor Bereket Habte Selassie, formerly chair of the Constitutional Commission of Eritrea and currently of the University of North Carolina. The membership of the Working Group includes a diverse group of experts in comparative constitutionalism, conflict resolution, development, political science, and sociology, and members of the donor community involved in assisting post-conflict societies.

A series of case studies papers has been commissioned on the constitutional processes of nearly 20 countries around the world. The Working Group is joined by relevant country and regional experts for its consideration of each case study. It is not anticipated that the series of case studies will produce a monolithic model for constitution-making. On the contrary, they will likely offer a range of different and perhaps even inconsistent approaches, the use of which will depend on the various social, cultural, political and economic conditions existing in a particular country. Through this process, the Working Group is attempting to discern the variables that underlie these different approaches, evaluate their respective effects, and, by applying a uniform analytical framework across a broad range of cases, derive common lessons regarding the complex process of constitution-making and national reconciliation.

Begun in 1991, the current phase of the *Project on Constitution-Making and National Reconciliation* is anticipated to be completed in early 2003. A final report will incorporate an assessment and synthesis of lessons learned, the identification of pitfalls to be avoided when constitution-making occurs in the aftermath of violent conflict, and the articulation of practical guidelines to be considered in the design of post-conflict constitution-making processes in the future, to maximize the potential of these processes in the consolidation and maintenance of peace.

The project includes an examination of constitution-making processes in the following countries:

> Bosnia and Herzegovina; Brazil; Cambodia; Colombia; East Timor; Eritrea; Ethiopia; Fiji; Hungary; Namibia; Nicaragua; Poland; South Africa; Spain; Uganda; Venezuela; Zimbabwe.

The following is an inventory of the issues to be considered in each of the case studies:

I. General Issues Pertaining to Conflict Resolution and Constitution-Making

What ramifications does the nature, duration, and intensity of the conflict, and the character of its termination, have for the constitution-making process? What are the limitations on using the constitution-making process as a means of conflict resolution and peace building? How should those involved in the constitution-making process evaluate which post-conflict issues are not appropriate for resolution through the constitution-making process and are best left to political negotiation? Are there circumstances in which constitutional reform would be preferable to creating a wholly new constitution? How is that determined? To what extent does the constitution-making process need to be coordinated with other post-conflict political negotiations that may deal with some of the same issues that will arise in the constitutional context?

From the perspective of building a stable peace, are there different dynamics between constitution-making in a post-independence scenario (i.e., drafting a new country's first constitution) and replacement of an existing constitution? How and to what extent have previous exercises in constitution-making included the use of negotiation techniques? What lessons can be drawn regarding the integration of traditional, indigenous methods of conflict resolution and public deliberation into the constitution-making process? How should those involved in the process determine whether to refer to the former constitution as a starting point or to intentionally begin with a blank slate? In those cases where a settlement agreement formed the basis of the constitutional process, are there steps which were taken or procedures followed in the establishment of the settlement agreement that recommend themselves for use in future constitutional processes? In what types of cases should constitution-making be anticipated and incorporated into the peace agreement, in the form of constitutional principles, a timetable for constitution-making, or mandating the structure of the process? Shaping the constitution-making process as an exercise in political negotiation and compromise risks producing a short-term accord at the expense of building strong democratic institutions and longterm stability. How can this be avoided?

II. Structure of the Process

Numerous choices need to be made with respect to establishment of a constitution-making authority that may impact on its relationship to post-conflict peace-building. Should a constitutional commission be established to organize the broader constitution-making process, including public education and consultation, and the actual drafting of the document? Alternatively, should a country move directly to a constitutional convention or similar process? Who should determine the mandate, timetable and rules of a constitutional commission or constituent assembly? Should the process include the election of a constituent assembly or a constitutional convention? Are there circumstances where an ordinary parliamentary assembly could be used for this purpose? Who will actually draft the constitution? Should a smaller committee be designated for this task? How will the drafters be chosen? To the extent that elections are held for a constitutional convention, what electoral systems should be employed, and how will the choice of electoral systems in the constitutional process affect the choice of future electoral systems? Should there be any provisions for judicial or other review of the actions of the constitution-making body?

III. Public Participation in the Process

Some recent constitutional processes which have attempted to address societal conflict have placed a fair amount of emphasis on public participation. In considering the potential costs and benefits of public participation in the constitution-making process, there are a number of questions and issues which arise. Should the process, for example, include one or more plebiscites which will allow the public to decide basic constitutional issues prior to the preparation of the draft constitution and/or to approve or reject the final document? Should there be public fora and/or formal arrangements for submission of comments by members of the public? If there are to be public fora for consultation and input, at what stages should they occur (e.g. before the beginning of the drafting process, following the completion of an initial draft or a draft of basic principles, or during the course of the drafting process.)? Should there be a program of public education associated with public participation, and, if so, what should that program entail? Should it include public education on the democratic principles and international human rights norms that need to be incorporated into the constitutional framework? Should the process of public consultation and participation facilitate the public airing of grievances by different groups in order to factor these issues as appropriate into constitutional deliberations? As part of the public education process, should this include exposure of each group within society to the needs and grievances of the others? What unofficial function(s) should be played by civil society during the course of the constitution-making process? Also, how important is the formal inclusion of civil society groups in the official process? Should certain sectors or institutions (e.g., the military, the church) be formally represented in—or intentionally excluded from—the official process?

On the other hand, the question of public participation raises the basic question of its scope and limitations. A balance may need to be achieved between the desire for completing the process expeditiously and the concern for the democracy of the process since public participation and public education may serve to prolong it. Are there circumstances in which, to advance the interests of short-term peace-building or long-term democratization, less public participation in (and pressure on) the constitution-making process would be preferable, confining the process—or at least certain parts of it—to a more restricted group of elites? Under what conditions is a more participatory process likely to produce a constitution that is democratic and protective of human rights and the rule of law—or less so? Are there measures that should be considered to ensure that the public participation component does not result in unrealistic public expectations or assumptions about the constitution-making process and the resulting document? What are the main principles or issues that the public should appropriately discuss and decide? Are there some less appropriate for this public approach? Should the public be involved in the final adoption or ratification process? Who should decide the level and structure of public participation? Finally, in connection with all of these issues, it is important to consider the extent to which the ultimate legitimacy of the constitution will depend upon the scope of the public participation in the process.

IV. Democratic Representation

Just as the scope of public participation raises the question of the ultimate legitimacy of the process, so does the issue of designated representatives and the method of their selection. Should the composition of a post-conflict constituent assembly reflect the distribution of power between political parties in parliament, or the ethnic, religious, or regional make-up of the country, or simply the results of a popular vote for this purpose? What role should political parties play in this process? What steps are appropriate to prevent an existing or transitional government from dominating or controlling the constitution-making process? To what extent, and how, should the constitution-making process ensure the representation and protection of minority interests? How can the guaranteed participation of specific ethnic, religious or political groups in the constitutional commission or convention be reconciled with democratic principles or conflict reduction, particularly if similar guarantees are not established for all in countries that have large numbers of distinct groups? What are effective strategies to ensure that the resolution of ethnic conflict will not so overshadow other concerns in the process as to compromise its legitimacy or undermine the development of sustainable democratic institutions? Where the prior conflict has involved serious human rights abuses, should participants in the constitution-making process be vetted for their involvement in those abuses? If so, how should the vetting be conducted? When factions or regions reject the peace settlement or the legitimacy of the new government and constitutional process, how should the constitution-making process deal with this refusal to participate?

V. The Timing and Sequencing of the Constitution-Making Process

The general issue of the timing and duration of the process may relate to the resolution of preexisting conflict. For example, are there any conditions precedent in the post-conflict phase for the constitution-making process to begin? Are time limits beneficial? A prolonged process may give an unfair advantage to a particular dominant faction thus leading to renewed conflict. On the other hand, it may permit other parties to build their strength and become better positioned to engage in constitutional discussions. Are there circumstances in which, from a conflict resolution perspective, a fast or attenuated constitution-making process is preferable? Do lessons emerge from previous cases of transitional constitution-making with respect to the sequencing of steps in the process? In addition, if the process includes the preparation of one or more drafts of the constitution, at what stage(s) in the process should those drafts be prepared and presented? If the process will include plebiscites, when should the plebiscites occur? If a constituent assembly is used, when in the constitutional process should it be elected? If the constitutional process is the product of a peace agreement, to what extent should the peace agreement determine the sequencing of the events in the process? Are there circumstances where it may be preferable to adopt a transitional charter which represents the establishment of consensus with regard to certain constitutional issues while postponing the consideration of more contentious issues to a future date?

In some cases, secessionist or opposition groups initiate a constitution-making process prior to independence or a transition, i.e., while the conflict is still ongoing. What are the dynamics of this process? When is an international role at this stage helpful and when can it exacerbate conflict?

VI. The Role of the International Community

Countries emerging from violent conflict will almost always need to depend upon the international community to varying degrees for the resources—financial, technical, and human—which will be necessary in order to conduct the constitution-making process. In some cases, a role for the international community in the constitutional process may result from its role in brokering a peace agreement. International involvement in the constitutional process may also contribute to international recognition of a newly independent state or acceptance of a new regime's legitimacy. On the other hand, the legitimacy of the constitutional process may be undermined where the international community is perceived as attempting to impose the process or result.

What are the variables that determine the appropriate role for the international community in terms of conflict reduction or the legitimacy of the process? To avoid the perception of foreign domination of the process, how important is it for international assistance to incorporate a multi-disciplinary approach that includes the consideration of sociological and cultural factors? Should the international community play any role in the selection of the participants in the process, including the possible vetting of participants where appropriate in the aftermath of serious human rights abuses? If so, how? What forms and methods of foreign assistance to the constitution-making process are most, and least, helpful? In the case of secession or the termination of occupation or colonization, is it helpful to have constitutional experts from the former ruling country involved in the process? What level of coordination is appropriate between the often multiple foreign actors who may even be providing assistance to different local factions in the constitution-making process?

Where the United Nations has become directly involved in mediating or resolving a conflict, the constitutional process may be dictated, at least in part, by UN resolutions. Under what circumstances should UN resolutions specifically mandate UN involvement in the constitution-making process? Similarly, are there circumstances in which regional inter-governmental organizations should become involved in the constitution-making process?

VII. The Role of International Law.

Are there emerging international norms relating to the constitution-making process or relating to the substance of any constitution? If so, how should these standards be determined and integrated? Several recent constitutions explicitly deal with the status of international law relative to domestic law and also directly incorporate international human rights standards into the constitution. Particularly in a post-conflict context, where concerns regarding the rights of various parties and contested international legal claims may be crucial to the consolidation of peace, how should these issues be addressed in the constitution-making process? Who should decide?

VIII. Essential Issues of Substance

Certain fundamental issues, such as the power and status to be accorded to geographic subdivisions, and the centralization or devolution of power, may be so integral to the construction of a stable peace as to be inseparable from an examination of the constitution-making process. When, how and by whom should such basic issues should be decided? Some modern constitutions contain certain immutable principles that are designed both to preserve the stability of the regime and to ensure against the recurrence of past abuses. Should a postconflict constitution include such immutable principles? If so, how should the constitution-making process determine such principles?

○